THE EXPERT'S GUIDE TO

marathon training

HUGH JONES

CARLTON
BOOKS

Contents

Introduction

Running comes naturally to most children, and I was no different. But I soon realised the satisfaction I could get by running further and faster. I hope you will feel the same way.

I took up running before I knew I had. It was impatience. Going to (and more particularly returning from) primary school in north-west London just wasn't quick enough at walking pace. Not only that, but I did the return journey in double-quick time during dinner hour. It was a good few years before I realised that this was more than a habit – it was the basic conditioning which primed me for a lifetime in sport. At the age of 11, in a Boy Scouts' cross-country race around a windswept reservoir, I finished ahead of older kids without making anything more than a casual effort. It was only then that I knew I had a talent.

While talent may allow you to be top dog in your secondary school, it doesn't necessarily mean much in national terms. It took several years before I bothered to do anything as disciplined as training. When I did (I was 16 and joined a running club), it still didn't mean anything much more formal than an upgrade of my toddler's trots of ten years before. Then, towards the end of my time at university, I brought more structure to the training. This was with the idea of running my second marathon, in June 1979. My first had been little more than a stab in the dark. The methodical application of training knowledge (not my own) brought on my form more generally, and within a year I ran for England in the World Cross-Country Championships.

A year later I won the AAA Marathon Championship, an old-style race of three laps around country lanes with a total field of 65. That race made me realise that marathon running was where my future lay, and I had already seen what benefits dedicated training could bring, in improving my time by five minutes each year. And after another year I knocked another five minutes off.

That was through the streets of London in the 1982 London Marathon. It was a far cry from the back lanes of a year previously. Vast crowds and TV coverage lent a feverish buzz to the occasion. My final burst over Westminster Bridge to the finish line was shown on the national evening news.

What had started for me not five miles away, twenty years before, had turned into a national event – of which I was at the forefront. The marathon has continued to grow in terms of people participating, and in terms of the public attention it commands. What was once seen as the errant pastime of a few eccentrics is now recognised as a meaningful challenge for anyone who cares to put him- or herself to the test.

I had never thought of it in these terms, but it had been true all along. It continues to be true for me today, long after the time when I can realistically challenge myself to perform better than before. That's not the nature of the challenge. The challenge is knowing that you have something – a capability – within yourself, and striving to give form to it in the most basic terms; distance travelled in time elapsed.

Expressed like this, running yields ruthlessly blunt results. That is the beauty and the appeal of it. Running itself isn't complicated, it merely requires will and application, and a little creativity in managing it alongside other commitments. Where it becomes complicated is in the reactions it engenders, although the underlying theme is gratifying reward for honest efforts. These come with your own body as the only mediator. In what other walk of life is the relation so direct?

When you make the effort to start training, this is what will strengthen your resolve. You will be able to see the difference. You will see your capabilities improve. If you follow the guidelines in the introductory chapters of this book you will be well prepared to embark on the training programme outlined in the diary section (Chapter 6). As you work your way through the sixteen weeks of the log, making notes of your training as you go, you will be able to see your personal progress in the most graphic way. You will be able to look back with satisfaction at what you have already achieved. This in itself will help inspire you to keep to the overall ambition you have set yourself.

Good running, and good luck.

Hugh Jones
London 2003

THE ANTARCTICA MARATHON IS ONE OF THE MOST GRUELLING RACES ON THE PLANET – BUT THE REWARDS ARE TREMENDOUS.

1
History of the Marathon

The marathon as we know it is little more than 100 years old, but there have been forms of long-distance races since the time of the ancient Egyptians. These days it is accessible to more people than ever.

It has been an Olympic distance since the modern Olympics started in 1896, but nothing like it was ever seen in the ancient Olympics, run from 776BC to 261AD. The longest race was less than 5km (3 miles). The marathon was adopted as a central part of the modern Olympic programme, and takes place in countless cities all over the world today, purely because of its popular appeal to the imagination.

Humans had once habitually run distances far greater than a marathon. As a hunter, one of man's greatest assets was his stamina. He would run his prey ragged. The hunted animal would bound away to apparent safety, only for the dogged hunter to turn up alongside again. This would go on until the animal, squandering its energy in nervous bursts, was too exhausted to resist.

A NINETEENTH-CENTURY ENGRAVING OF THE ROMANTIC SCHOOL DEPICTING THE DEATH OF PHEIDIPPIDES AFTER SUPPOSEDLY RUNNING FROM MARATHON TO ATHENS WITH NEWS OF THE GREEK ARMY'S VICTORY OVER THE PERSIANS AROUND 490BC (FROM THE RISCHGITZ COLLECTION).

Such obvious purpose to running was undermined as weaponry became more sophisticated, and humans able to kill at remote distance. In Egyptian times running ability was prized as a military skill. King Taharka instituted a long distance race specifically to keep his army up to scratch. The distance was coincidentally close to 100km (62 miles), contested today as the standard "ultradistance" event. The race itself has been revived in recent years as the "Pharaonic 100km" from the Sakkara Pyramids south west of Cairo to the Hawara Pyramid at El Faiyum.

The most accomplished runners, both within the military and in civilian society, served as messengers up to the beginning of the nineteenth century and, over rough country, were better than a horse.

The tale upon which the modern Olympic marathon rests is the mythic run of Pheidippides from Marathon to Athens. He was a professional messenger and, in 490BC, is supposed to have brought a message from the plains of Marathon, where the Greek Army had just won a crucial battle against the invading Persian Army of General Datis. After the battle, in which he may have taken part, and possibly even been wounded, he was dispatched to Athens to deliver the news: "Rejoice, we are victorious". He did this and no more, dropping dead with the delivery.

There are many variations of this story, most of them more plausible than this version. The Greeks may have been victorious, but the battle had not been conclusive, as the rest of the Greek Army was marching towards Athens to forestall another Persian landing much closer to the city. The most contemporaneous historian, Herodotus, wrote 50 years later that Pheidippides had been sent from Athens to Sparta, before the battle, to request help. He does not mention whether Pheidippides returned with the Spartan reply (which was no). The "Spartathlon" race, which is held today over a distance of 240km (149 miles), commemorates this slightly more likely version of events.

Likely or not, Pheidippides' death run from Marathon to Athens was incorporated into a poem by Robert Browning, and this accounts for the currency it had at the time Baron Pierre de Coubertin was attempting to resurrect the Olympic Games for the modern era.

De Coubertin was a Frenchman, who had grown up at a time of national shame. Trounced in the Franco-Prussian War, the French had lost national territory, been forced to pay reparations and forbidden a national army while Prussian troops occupied the country. There followed a civil war which further weakened French national standing. De Coubertin sought reasons for this weakness, and the apparent strength of France's rival powers, Britain and Prussia.

He latched on to Britain's public

schools, and in particular their emphasis on sporting endeavour, as a crucial factor in building national character. On a tour of Britain, he met William Brookes, founder of the Much Wenlock Olympic Society, which had already held its inaugural event in 1850, followed up in 1859 and 1885. De Coubertin attempted both to make sport compulsory in French schools and to promote an international sporting festival also based upon the ancient Olympics.

He launched his Olympic campaign in 1892, and two years later formed the International Olympic Committee at the Sorbonne. The delegates agreed to promote the first modern Olympics in 1896 in Athens, and subsequently at intervals of four years. One of the delegates was Michel Bréal, who argued

APRIL 1896: THIS PAINTING SHOWS SPIRIDON LOUIS OF GREECE WINNING THE FIRST OLYMPIC MARATHON. HE IS ACCOMPANIED OVER THE FINAL METRES IN THE ARENA BY THE HEIRS TO THE GREEK THRONE, PRINCES GEORGE AND CONSTANTINE.

for a long-distance race as one of the events, and dusted off the hoary old story of Pheidippides in support. He carried his argument, but the Greek government also had to be convinced that the Olympics should be held at all.

As has happened so often since, the authorities saw the Olympics as a means by which to galvanise national feeling. The Royal family became involved and contributions from the Greek diaspora poured in. Vast sums were expended in building a marble replica of the stadium at Olympia, and the first Olympic Marathon was run from Marathon Bridge to this stadium in Athens, over a distance of 40km (25 miles).

In the months leading up to the Olympic race, there were several attempts to run this course. In February 1896, two runners departed from Athens and completed the distance, but one of them, foreshadowing many similar instances, took a ride for part of the way. A month before the Olympic race, a Greek Championship event was held, in which 11 competitors ran from Marathon to Athens. This was the first ever marathon race. Two weeks later there was another, billed as an official trial and attracting 38 entrants. The winner recorded 3:11.27 and a water-carrier named Spiridon Louis finished fifth in 3:18:27. On a separate occasion at that time two women, Melpomene and Stamatis Rovithi, were also reported to have run from Marathon to Athens.

Eighteen men lined up at the start of the Olympic Marathon on 10 April 1896. Of the four foreign runners only Gyula Kellner, a Hungarian, had run the distance before as a time trial. The three others had run in the middle distances at the Games and were chancing to little more than luck that they would stay the course.

The Greek organisers seemed better prepared, and had already made some arrangements which remain as standard practice to this day: refreshment stations

SPIRIDON LOUIS: THE GREEK WINNER OF THE FIRST OLYMPIC MARATHON IN 1896.

were dotted along the course, a cavalry officer acted as lead vehicle and soldiers were used as race marshals to keep the public off the course and assist stricken competitors. Personal drinks were allowed, to be administered by the runner's own assistant: drug testing was only introduced many decades later and performance-affecting substances were consumed with gusto, but probably to little benefit.

The three foreign middle-distance runners lasted surprisingly well, retiring at 23km (14 miles), 32km (20 miles) and 37km (23 miles). Spiridon Louis had taken the lead from the last of these, the Australian Edwin Flack, at about 33km (20½ miles). The starter, one Colonel Papadiamantopoulos, who seemed to be acting as race referee, then rode ahead to inform the waiting crowd in the

stadium. Louis did not disappoint, and led by a literal mile as he entered the stadium to win in a time of 2:58:50. Greeks took second and third, until Kellner, who had come in fourth, protested that the third Greek, Spiridon Belokas, had taken a ride – something that was almost becoming common practice. Nine runners finished the race.

The marathon was now established, perhaps better established than the Olympics themselves, whose next two showings in Paris and St Louis, bordered on the farcical. The next marathon was held only two months later, from Paris to the outlying town of Conflans.

A century before, once running had ceased to be the most efficient means of relaying messages, those wealthy people who had employed couriers had found another purpose to running. It provided an ideal spectacle upon which to lay bets. Races were arranged solely for this purpose throughout most of the nineteenth century. In Britain, after about 1860, gentlemen's "Hare and Hounds" or "Harrier" running clubs were formed, mainly for paperchasing, an early version of cross-country running.

The clubs were put under the regulation of the Amateur Athletic Association, formed in Oxford in 1880. The very name advertised the disdain with which they viewed the betting fraternity and the "professional" runners. A stand-off developed in which de Coubertin was decidedly with the amateurs. An Italian had his entry to the inaugural Olympic Marathon turned down on the grounds that he was professional. But a marathon was as good a race on which to gamble as any other, perhaps more so, as its duration allowed for a greater repertoire of dirty tricks to be brought into play.

Paris-Conflans was a professional promotion, and offered a bonus for breaking Louis' Olympic time. An English builder, Len Hurst, collected the money by recording 2:31:30. The distance was

1908 OLYMPICS: DORANDO PIETRI OF ITALY IS HELPED OVER THE FINISHING LINE OF THE MARATHON IN LONDON, ONLY TO BE DISQUALIFIED. QUEEN ALEXANDRA WAS STILL IMPRESSED ENOUGH TO GIVE HIM A TROPHY.

quoted as 40km, but methods of measurement were unreliable and could be subject to the influence of ambitious organisers eager for fast times.

Over in the United States, the New York Athletic Club organised a marathon over 25 miles – almost an imperial conversion of the earlier races, being 40.23km. The groundbreaking nature of the race was demonstrated by only 10 of the 30-strong field finishing, the first of them in a time almost half an hour slower than Louis.

The runner who had retired at 23km in Athens was Arthur Blake, a member of the Boston Athletic Association who was not at all put off by his first abortive experience. Within a year, on 15 March 1897, the first of the BAA Boston Marathons was held. The race has been held every year since (except for 1918 when a military marathon relay

substituted), making Boston the oldest marathon race in the world.

Like the earlier New York race, it was run from point to point, mainly downhill from Ashland (it now starts a little further west in Hopkinton) to downtown Boston. The winner was the New York victor, John McDermott, who improved to 2:55:10 – although the course length was given as 39km (24 miles).

Apart from Boston, most marathons continued to be held over 40km or 25 miles, including both the Paris and St Louis Olympic races – although the St Louis race, exceptionally, turned out to be overdistance. Races spread to South Africa and England, the host country for the 1908 Olympics.

The Franco-British Exhibition was being held at the new White City stadium in West London, where the Olympic Marathon was to finish in front of the royal box from which Queen Alexandra would watch. Preserving the royal theme, the start was to be at Windsor Castle. The length was fixed at 26 miles (41.8km) and seems to have been measured very conscientiously. A

late request from the Queen to move the start back, to the East Lawn of Windsor Castle, from where it could be seen by the royal children in their nursery, added a further 385 yards (352m).

Those 385 yards proved too much for the first over the finishing line, the Italian Dorando Pietri. Pietri had run a relatively steady race, although nearly all runners started at a furious pace (the leaders passing 10 miles within 57 minutes). By the last few miles the pace of most runners was at least two minutes slower per mile. Shortly before entering the stadium Pietri finally overtook the South African Charles Hefferon, who had led the race from 15 miles. Catching the leader proved too much, and on the track Pietri staggered and fell four times before being assisted over the finishing line by race officials. The race was awarded to an American, Johnny Hayes, who finished without "unfair" assistance 32 seconds later.

Pietri's distress was temporary, and he recovered quickly. Less fortunate was a Portuguese competitor in the following Olympics held in Stockholm. Twenty-year-old Francisco Lazaro was three times national champion and possessed a doctor's certificate pronouncing him fit to run the marathon. But marathon day dawned hot, and the race was set off at 13.45 in the full glare of the sun. Lazaro reached 30km (18 miles) before he collapsed, and was taken to hospital. Suffering from heat exhaustion, he died the following day. This is the only instance of death in Olympic marathons, although fatalities in mass participation marathons do occur. In several countries race organisers now require medical certificates, much as Lazaro had produced, before confirming any entrant.

The specific marathon distance determined so haphazardly in London was eventually adopted as the official length of a marathon, but not until 16 years later. The distance stands today in metric form as 42,195m. Meanwhile, marathons continued to be run at varying distances,

JIM PETERS APPROACHES THE POLYTECHNIC STADIUM EN ROUTE TO ONE OF HIS THREE WORLD RECORDS AT THIS EVENT.

the longest of which was probably the 1920 Olympic marathon in Antwerp, at 42,750m (26.5 miles).

Another consequence of the London Olympics was that the British, disappointed by the poor performances of their runners (who had led the mad charge out of Windsor), held an annual Polytechnic Marathon, named after the organising club, over the same course. This became the stage for many world-beating performances, from the inaugural race in 1909 (Harry Barrett, 2:42:31) through the golden years of Jim Peters (1951–54, during which he reduced the world record to 2:20:43, 2:18:41 and then 2:17:40) to the 1960s (1963 Basil Heatley 2:14:26; 1964 Buddy Edelen, 2:13:55; 1965 Morio Shigematsu, 2:12:00).

Apart from the Olympic Marathon and Boston, there were few other significant races established before the Second World War. The Kosice Marathon in Slovakia, founded in 1924, is still run today and has taken over from "The Poly" as the oldest marathon in Europe.

THE KOSICE PEACE MARATHON: RUNNERS SET OFF AT THE BEGINNING OF EUROPE'S OLDEST MARATHON, IN PRESENT-DAY SLOVAKIA, IN 1948.

RACE OFFICIAL, JACK SEMPLE, IN STREET CLOTHES, TRIES TO PULL KATHERINE SWITZER (261) OUT OF THE 1967 BOSTON MARATHON, AS THE MALE RUNNERS AROUND HER MOVE IN TO FORM A PROTECTIVE CURTAIN.

After 1945, marathons were started in Japan at Fukuoka (1947), Twente in Holland (1948) and the Athens Classical Marathon was resurrected over the original 1896 course (with an additional 2,195m/2,400 yards) in 1955.

The Japanese took to marathon running with enthusiasm, and by the 1960s the Fukuoka race was indisputably the best in the world. It was an élite race, featuring the top Japanese and a few runners invited from overseas, and drew widespread public attention. Other races at this time may have had more runners, although none had more than a few hundred, but no other had the quality of Fukuoka. Toru Terasawa had already run 2:16:19 in 1962, but in 1967 the Australian Derek Clayton reduced the record to 2:09:37.

Clayton purportedly beat his own world record time in 1969 in Antwerp,

recording 2:08:33.6. The figures had a spurious accuracy to them. Doubts about the accuracy of the course have never been resolved, since the method of measurement employed by the organisers, the average of car odometer readings, is known to be unreliable.

At the same time as top marathon runners were beginning to run inside 5-minute mile pace for the distance, the

FRED LEBOW, NEW YORK ROAD RUNNERS CLUB PRESIDENT (LEFT), GIVES VIETNAM VET BOB WIELAND HIS MARATHON MEDAL.

seeds of a popular revolution were being planted. A New Yorker, Fred Lebow, organised a marathon on a shoestring, comprising a short lap to start, and then four full laps of Central Park. Attracting little over 100 runners, it was no different to many other races at the time, struggling to find the space on the road, a modest budget and enough competitors to make it all worthwhile.

The number of runners grew slowly but steadily, and Lebow secured a sponsorship deal with Olympic Airlines for the 1973 race. Frank Shorter's win in the 1972 Olympics had raised the profile of marathon running in the USA, and by 1975 participation had risen to 500, although the Boston Marathon had already grown to accommodate 1,800 runners. The sponsorship was not renewed, and Lebow was thrown back onto his own initiative.

The American Bicentennial fell in 1976, and Lebow used his connections with City Hall to move the marathon out of Central Park and run it through the five boroughs of the city. The big city marathon was born. The route started at the Staten Island end of the Verazzano

Narrows Bridge and ran through all the various ethnic districts of Brooklyn before crossing into Queens at halfway, and then over the 59th Street Bridge after 25km (15½ miles). Up First Avenue for 5km (3 miles) before passing into the Bronx, runners then returned to Manhattan on Fifth Avenue through Harlem, turning into Central Park only for the final 5km. Shorter himself lined up for this race, alongside Bill Rodgers who had won the Boston Marathon in 1975 and now recorded the first of four consecutive wins in New York.

Some 1,500 more finished behind Rogers in the first ever marathon race for the masses. A new era had begun as cities elsewhere in the world aspired to emulate Lebow's achievement in putting the marathon at the forefront of public attention. People couldn't help but notice the new phenomenon when it took place through the centre of the cities in which they lived.

Berlin established not just a city-wide marathon, in 1980, but also a 25km

GRETE WAITZ WINS THE 1980 NEW YORK MARATHON IN RECORD TIME.

race on a different date. The London Marathon was first held in 1981 after Chris Brasher, overwhelmed by his experience of the 1979 New York Marathon, resolved to organise

something similar in London. The race grew from 7,000 runners in the first year to leapfrog New York's numbers by the second, as 16,000 runners finished the race.

Suddenly, no major world city was complete without its own marathon, and a lot of minor cities got in on the act, too. Inclusiveness was the watchword, as many cities tried using marathons to boost their tourist industries. In a marked turnaround from pre-New York days, women, as well as men, were welcome.

The 1967 Boston Marathon had gained notoriety when an official tried to eject a woman in mid-race (Katherine Switzer, who had entered under her initial and surname only). Although the attempt was unsuccessful, few other marathons at the time were more accommodating. A few women had run the distance over the years, particularly from the early 1960s, but no international championship incorporated a women's marathon.

The burgeoning mass marathon

6 NOVEMBER 1994: THE TWENTY-FIFTH NEW YORK MARATHON GETS OFF TO A GOOD START FROM STATEN ISLAND, NEW YORK.

movement changed all that. New York admitted women from the inaugural 1970 race, and Boston followed suit in 1972, as women increasingly moved centre stage. The Norwegian Grete Waitz, on the verge of retiring from competition at shorter distances, ran New York in 1978 and set a truly respectable women's record of 2:32:30. She reduced it to 2:27:33 in 1979 and 2:25:41 in 1980.

In September 1982, the European Championships incorporated a women's marathon for the first time, won by Rosa Mota in 2:36:04 over the classic Marathon to Athens route. Mota finished third in the inaugural women's Olympic Marathon in Los Angeles two years later, behind Joan Benoit's 2:24:52 and Waitz's 2:26:18. Fourth in that race was Waitz's compatriot Ingrid Kristiansen, who established a record of 2:21:06 the

following year in London, which stood for 13 years.

Derek Clayton's disputed men's record from Antwerp nearly survived that long, until Alberto Salazar broke it by 20 seconds in winning the 1981 New York Marathon. Unfortunately, when this course was finally checked by relatively newly accepted, accurate methods in 1985, it was found to be short by about 150m (164 yards). Rob DeCastella, from Australia had run 2:08:18 in Fukuoka six weeks after Salazar's performance. Welshman Steve Jones shaved 12 seconds off DeCastella's time in the 1984 Chicago Marathon, although Portugal's Carlos Lopes, who had won the Olympic race that year, brought the time down to 2:07:12 in Rotterdam six months later.

Current records stand at 2:05:38 to Khalid Kannouchi in the 2002 London Marathon, and 2:15:25 to Paula Radcliffe in the 2003 London Marathon. Radcliffe's time is perhaps of more significance, as it reflects the growing competitiveness of women's marathon running. Waitz, Kristiansen and Mota were lonely pioneers – Rosa Mota won the 1987 World Championships (at which Kristiansen won the 10,000m) by a margin of 2km. Radcliffe is also out on her own, but not by that much, as Catherine Ndereba and Naoko Takahashi have also broken 2:20, 50 years after Jim Peters did so.

There are many other women close to this barrier, and many of them are Kenyan. Another significant trend in the 1990s was towards Kenyan, and to a lesser extent Ethiopian, domination of men's and women's distance running. Part of the explanation is the globalisation of a sport, freed from its amateur past, which offers rich rewards to those who excel.

But there are rewards of a different kind for all participants in the marathon. Quite what they are is sometimes hard to define. But that is what we will consider next.

14 APRIL 2002: KHALID KHANNOUCHI BREAKS THE WORLD RECORD IN LONDON.

13 APRIL 2003: PAULA RADCLIFFE OF GREAT BRITAIN WINS THE 2003 FLORA LONDON MARATHON IN WORLD RECORD TIME.

2
Why run a Marathon?

Maybe that's too tough a question. Let's break it down: firstly consider "why run?" then why you may want to run a marathon. But if that's marathons in the plural, maybe you are already hooked.

Why run?

There are almost as many reasons why people run as there are people who run. Everyone who does has good reasons. If running is habitual, then the reasons for it may not even be considered. If there weren't any though, people would soon grind to a halt.

The original reason humans ran was to hunt down prey. It's highly unlikely many people still do it on that account. Even the later purpose, to run messages, has been overtaken by technology. Yet there are still occasions on which the ability to transfer yourself from one place to another, under your own power, is very useful. We only have to suffer a train strike to realise this.

Many runners today have re-entered the sport, after absences stretching back to schooldays, on the basis of a bet. How long it takes to get to the local newsagent and back, whether it's still possible to run under eight minutes for a single mile, whether it's possible to run three miles without stopping, whether you can beat the bus over six stops through traffic.

These kinds of questions may be worth putting to the test, but they are usually the sort of questions which demand an instant answer, more likely than not before the pubs close. There's no time to improve the odds by doing some training beforehand. That means that the first taste of sport after a long absence can be a painful experience.

Our bodies were built to run, but in many cases we have just let them run down. They are no longer conditioned for it. Jolting them back into action is neither a pleasurable nor an effective way to proceed. With a little gentle coaxing the lost reflexes can be reactivated. The body responds with an intuition beyond mere school memories. It is doing what it was designed to do, among other things.

Motivation

The professional runners of the nineteenth century were trained, but their motivation was purely to win. Money and fame were the spoils of victory – just as they are today, and the monetary rewards for the world's absolute best are higher now than they have ever been before. This is not something that can motivate very many of us. We sense that we are not one of the chosen few, and indeed, the odds of that are stacked against us.

When all the big reasons to run have been chiselled away, the central core of private motivation remains. This was the concern of Pierre de Coubertin before he got involved in setting up the Olympics. Like many Victorians, he saw the fate of society resting on the sum of individual motivations. He sought to engineer a social outcome by re-educating individuals.

De Coubertin saw the moral and physical wellbeing of France as something that could be brought about by prescribing sport among schoolboys (the Victorians were less concerned about schoolgirls). Sport was seen as the ideal tonic for building character. Compulsion is usually what ruins things and the most successful gentlemen sportsmen, who performed their feats in parallel with the professionals, were self-motivated. Corny though it sounds, the

BARON PIERRE DE COUBERTIN, THE FOUNDER OF THE MODERN OLYMPIC GAMES.

masses who take up running today have more in common with the Corinthian ideals of amateurism than they may realise.

Even those runners who win are unlikely to be primarily motivated by money. They have arrived in that position, through years of training, without clairvoyance. During all those years, their motivation came from within themselves, a personal curiosity to see what they could do. When winners start to lose, then maybe their demise is hastened by the lessening ability to win money (and the search for alternative means of income), but most remain as runners. It is a sport primarily of personal reward.

Benefits

Just as people don't give up smoking simply because it would be better for them, they don't often start running for that reason either. Even so, it's true. The body's response when you start to run is to adapt itself to this new, or rediscovered purpose. Medical benefits inevitably follow. When you first run, you get out of breath over any distance. Unfit people comment with wonder on marathon finishers: "and he/she wasn't even out of breath". This is only one of the effects of training.

When you run, your body needs to deliver oxygen to the muscles via your blood. Running stimulates the body's entire oxygen delivery system. The lungs draw deeper. The heart pumps more strongly and each stroke is at a greater volume. The resting pulse rate lowers. The capillaries penetrate more finely into the muscle tissue.

The outward appearance of your body also responds to the demands of training. You need more energy and your body will burn fat reserves to acquire it.

AT AN EARLY AGE CHILDREN RUN NATURALLY. CONTINUING TO RUN LATER IN LIFE REQUIRES MORE DELIBERATE PLANNING.

Muscles are simultaneously strengthened and, because they are heavier than fat, this may counteract an overall tendency to lose weight. But the distribution of weight does change, along with the definition and tone of the musculature.

As the body absorbs the stresses of training and adapts to them, it becomes more resilient. Colds may still come and go, but in general the body is more resistant to illness and less severely affected by common ailments. The one area in which the body may become more vulnerable is physical injury – but

RUNNERS IN THE MARATONA DELLA CITTÀ DI ROMA PASS VICTOR EMMANUEL'S MONUMENT AND THE CAMPODOGLIO.

these are often minor muscular problems which can be simply treated.

Does running give you a longer life? Certainly the medical benefits of running lead to a reduced risk of heart disease, high blood pressure and diabetes. Running also gives you a life longer on quality. In old age, continued physical activity becomes increasingly synonymous with the quality of life.

There are other less direct benefits that running may bring about by changing life's habits. It can induce you to drink less alcohol and eat more healthily, simply as a reflexive expression of your body's requirements and your own changing preferences.

The psychological payoff from running comes very quickly. Immediately

there is a satisfaction in having overcome inertia – a sense of having achieved something. It may be raining outside and the warmth of home hard to leave, but it is almost unknown to return without feeling better for the outing. What you achieve is measurable. You can time yourself over a particular course. If you run that same course a month later, after steady training, you will see the improvement inscribed in the digits on your wristwatch.

Some people buy dogs as an excuse to get themselves out of the house. Running gives you that reason without all the added inconvenience and mess. Getting out into the open, as opposed to walking hurriedly from home to car, bus stop or train station, is something to be

savoured. We see things we otherwise wouldn't: the frosted trees, the ground fog and the rising sun.

Running gives you time to yourself. (There aren't a great many occasions during the working day when you can be alone and in a state of relaxation.) You are in command of your actions. There is no one to tell you what to do. You decide where to go. You have time to think. This in itself can be a great stress reliever, but it also allows you to develop a perspective on problems. The pattern of blood circulation while running doesn't allow you to think too deeply about other things, but it provides ideal conditions in which to mull them over. You can return from a run with new insights into particular problems.

As you get used to running, you develop a sixth sense of time, distance and pace. You appreciate the relation of time and distance through yourself as the medium by which they are related. This can be empowering in the most banal of situations. If the bus doesn't come, you know how long it will take to get to your destination relying on nothing but your own abilities.

Even money and fame, on a modest scale, may be within your reach. Races award age-group prizes, sometimes in both individual and team categories, and you may find that the occasional shoe voucher comes your way. Local papers usually cover sport for the participant more than for the spectator, so you stand a good chance of getting a mention.

It is closer to home where it really counts. Most people take up running in their thirties or forties, often when they have young children of their own. It is one of the best examples you can give. There is no need to get children to run – at an early age they will do that as a matter of course – but your own example gives silent encouragement for them to continue with it more deliberately when they might otherwise have outgrown their youthful exuberance. At the very

minimum, they will grow up more aware of what they can do.

What you can do is the most central question. After you start running, you can clearly see improvements from month to month, and measure progress. Sooner or later you will wonder how far this progress can be maintained. What can you do? What are your limits? This is not necessarily the moment at which you may decide to run a marathon. You may have reached a comfortable plateau of training. If so, and you wish to remain there, you may still see your performances improve over time.

Why a marathon?

Most people do things for a reason, but these may not necessarily be very well defined. A decision to run a marathon has some big implications, at least for the following few months, and perhaps indefinitely. Yet runners often slide into a marathon with very little thought.

Common reasons for deciding to run a marathon may include:

"Everyone else is doing one" By this you may mean that a few people you know have talked about running a marathon. You may be the only one of them who actually takes it through to a conclusion. If so, it says more about your own ambitions than what anyone else says or does.

"I've seen the London Marathon on TV, and it looks like a lark" The devil is in the detail. Over 30,000 people complete the London Marathon each year, and each one of them has a different experience. The attitude and preparedness of each runner varies greatly. The key to success lies in blending each of these attributes so that you can sustain an enjoyable experience through the duration of the race.

"If the rhino man can do it, I can" Outward appearances can be deceptive. Cunningly disguised inside that costume there may be a seasoned marathon runner.

"I've tried every other distance" But did any of them feel like it was the right distance? Most people are not natural marathon runners – they are likely to be a lot better at 100m, a mile or 5 miles. If you find your performances improve as the distance over which you have raced gets longer, then maybe the marathon is the event for you.

"I'll just do one, to raise money for charity" This is not a good reason in itself. If charity is the motivator, it would be better to do the fundraising for someone else who wants to do the running.

"It's a challenge" It is.

None of these reasons for trying a marathon is unworthy. It's just that it is a big decision and bears thinking about at some length. Don't enter a big marathon just to be accepted where others are rejected, or to get one over on others – like the person inside the rhino suit. Running a marathon means many long hours of effort, even before race day comes around. If you have already started to run, you will appreciate more what a marathon may require of you. If you want to see what you can do based on experience in your training and in other races, then curiosity is as good a reason as any (I would say that – it was my first marathon motive).

A marathon may cement running into your life. It's a long-term thing, at least if you don't enter as a bet the night before (impossible now, but the current race director did just that in the first London Marathon). If you really want to get the best possible performance out of yourself, then it takes months of effort. Once you have made that effort, you may not want to see the effects seep away again.

Many people, when they finish their first marathon say "never again" as they cross the finish line, only to find themselves lining up for another one six months later. Careful: you could be letting yourself in for a life sentence.

3
Getting started

There is no time like the present for beginning your marathon training – in fact you may already *be* a runner, and not even be aware of it: ever tried running for a bus?

If you miss that bus, and then try to run on to catch it at the next stop, you are already well on the way, mentally and physically, to being a runner.

Running as a regular activity demands a certain resolve, but the investment of time, effort and money is all up to your own discretion. You can buy equipment as you go, and as you come to think that you really do need these items. Don't assume that you need to spend money as a "commitment" before starting to run. Above all, don't join a gym for the sake of using a shiny new running machine. The fees would keep most runners shod and clothed for several years.

Starting to run should be as easy a process as possible. Don't leap into action, no matter how much you don't want to miss the bus; take things slowly. Think of a local landmark, to which you feel you could run without stopping – it could be only 400 metres or yards away, like a post box or a paper shop (or a bus stop). Your first run should be to see if you can indeed run to it, at a pace of your own choosing. Once there, stop, turn around, and start to walk back. Once you feel recovered, start to jog again until you reach home.

What do you need for this first exploratory training session? You probably already possess a pair of training shoes, and T-shirts or sweatshirts can be pulled out of any old drawer. You can run this far quite comfortably in leisure shorts, or even jeans. If you are absolutely new to running, then your first few weeks will not involve the kind of distances that would cause you discomfort in this impromptu get-up. It has the added advantage of not marking you out as a "proper runner", in which role you may at first feel a little exposed.

Only when you can run further, will you need more specialist equipment, and at each stage it is you who is in the best position to decide what item would

be of most benefit. It should only take a couple of weeks, running every second day, before you are able to run to your selected landmark and back without walking at all, or feeling distressed. Then you can pick another landmark further afield, and repeat the process.

Shoes

Now you have tried out your existing shoes, do they feel as comfortable to run in as they are for walking? As you start to run you will have a different action and impose a different pattern of wear on

FEW CONDITIONS WILL STOP YOU FROM RUNNING. APART FROM ICE AND EXTREME HEAT AND COLD, YOU CAN CONQUER THE ELEMENTS AND FEEL BETTER FOR DOING SO.

the shoes. Training shoes last much longer if they are used only for walking, but outward wear is not the only sign to look for. The midsole, between the insole of the shoe and the outer tread, is made of compressible material to cushion the jarring of a runner's foot against the pavement. After a while this material loses its springiness, and with it its protective qualities. Once you resolve to persevere with running – beyond the first week or two – a pair of running shoes, used only for running, is probably the first purchase you will want to make.

Go to a newsagent, buy a running magazine, and look through the directory of specialist running shops. Many will be mail-order outlets, but these are for people who already know what model of shoe they want. You need to go to a specialist high-street running shop and ask the sales assistants for their advice. They will most likely be runners themselves, and more interested in keeping your custom in the future than making a quick one-off sale. In many cases they should let you briefly "test run" a pair of shoes to make sure you feel comfortable in them.

Shoes can incorporate different technical features appropriate to

RUNNING SHOES CAN INCORPORATE DIFFERENT FEATURES, AND STAFF AT SPECIALIST SHOPS CAN ADVISE YOU ON THESE.

SHOPPING

Your body changes throughout the day and, if you are planning to shop for shoes, you should wait until after midday when your feet may have swollen a bit and you can make sure they fit comfortably.

---

different kinds of runner. The main criteria are your weight and the way in which your foot moves as it strikes the ground. Ground contact is usually made from the outside of the heel, after which the foot rolls slightly inward, so that push off comes from the big toe. This rotational movement from the outside of the heel is called pronation. Shoes are made for normal pronators, over-pronators and under-pronators (who may be supinators, if the inside of their heel strikes the ground first, and they push off from outside of the foot). These are matters on which the sales assistants should be able to help.

Shoe companies produce shoes spread at carefully calculated intervals of a price range. You should find an appropriate pair somewhere in the middle of any particular company's range. It is rare that the most expensive shoe is the best one for you, but it's also unlikely that the cheapest will be. In all shoes there is a trade-off between the lightness of the shoe and the support that it can offer. Shoes in which you will be doing most of your training should be selected for comfort, support and cushioning. Relatively few runners buy a separate, lighter pair of shoes specifically for racing in.

Clothing

You may want to continue running incognito even after buying shoes specifically to run in. When your "landmark run" every other day reaches an out-and-back distance of a mile (1.5km) or more, you may find that leisure shorts start to chafe, or that you are sweating too much inside a pair of jeans. If so, you need to drop the civilian camouflage and come out into the open as a self-declared runner.

Once you do this, by buying a pair of running shorts, you will appreciate that their lightness, flexibility and water shedding or "hygroscopic" qualities make them far more comfortable. They don't cling to you when it's raining, or when you are sweating heavily. The air circulates more freely around your legs, allowing sweat to evaporate more easily. The material is soft enough not to chafe (although for very long distances you may need to take further precautions).

Even in winter, it may not be necessary to cover up your legs. They are the most active part of your body when you run, and keep warm through blood circulation. When the temperature drops below about 5ºC (41ºF), you may need to buy a pair of nylon leggings. The loose-fitting kind often known as "tracksters" serve the purpose well.

Equipment

These are the basic items that will allow you to keep on course, come rain or shine.

STOPWATCH
THE ONLY ESSENTIAL GADGET, TO KEEP TRACK OF YOUR TIME AND EFFORT. GO FOR ONE WITH A LARGE DISPLAY AND SPLIT-TIME FACILITY.

VEST
THE BASIC RACING ITEM – WORN OVER CLOTHING IF NECESSARY, OR PROVIDING AN INNER LAYER ON COLD DAYS.

SPORTS BRA

THERMAL TOP
A POLYPROPYLENE TOP WILL BE WATER-RESISTANT AND CONDUCT SWEAT AWAY FROM YOUR BODY – BUT OFFERS LITTLE WIND PROTECTION.

SHORTS
THESE OFFER FREEDOM OF MOVEMENT, BUT YOU MAY PREFER LYCRA CYCLING SHORTS.

BOTTOMS
ESSENTIAL FOR WINTER TRAINING. GO FOR 'ROADSTERS' OR 'TRACKSTERS' WHICH ARE NOT AS TIGHT AS TIGHTS OR AS HEAVY AS CONVENTIONAL TRACKSUIT BOTTOMS.

SOCKS
DOUBLE-LAYER SOCKS WILL REDUCE THE CHANCE OF GETTING BLISTERS.

TOP
GET A 'TECHNICAL' LONG-SLEEVED TOP SO THAT YOU CAN WEAR A THERMAL UNDERNEATH.

TRAINERS
TAKE ADVICE FROM SPECIALIST RUNNING SHOPS ABOUT WHICH MODEL IS BEST FOR YOU.

REPLACING SHOES

The regularity with which you replace worn shoes is important. As shoes wear, they offer less protection and support. Wearing worn-out shoes is a significant cause of injury.

On most days, an ordinary cotton T-shirt is the most comfortable thing you can wear on your upper body. If it's hot, your sweat may soak the cotton; if it's raining, the T-shirt will get soaked anyway. When it does, it will cling to your body and feel uncomfortable. To avoid this you can buy a polypropylene or other synthetic fibre T-shirt or vest which carries moisture away from your skin.

On other occasions the upper body can chill more quickly. The first precaution is to switch a short-sleeved T-shirt for a long-sleeved one. Forearms and wrists exposed in cold weather will quickly lose circulation. You may find that when you get back home you are unable to turn the key in the lock. To keep fingers warm, either buy a pair of gloves, use a spare pair of socks, or simply clasp the cuffs of long sleeves in your hands.

You can overcome the cold by adding layers of clothing, but you risk sweating too much. If you wear a water-repelling layer next to your skin, avoid wearing a second layer which traps the sweat inside. This may mean that the time has come to consider investing in one of the expensive Gore-tex jackets on the market. Of course, you might get by quite easily without one. It is possible, unless you run slowly up exposed mountainsides in your training.

In cold weather, you will lose most heat through your head. A thin woollen hat may be more than enough to protect you, and you may prefer to wear a headband instead. Ears will feel most chilled in driving rain, and your headgear should be able to cover them. A baseball cap is an item I would go far to avoid wearing, but a peaked hat can provide your face with effective protection from driving rain.

Socks have so far only been mentioned as substitute gloves. Any old pair will do for this purpose, but there are now specialist running socks available which are not mere gimmicks – they offer definite advantages. Cotton socks suffer the same disadvantages as T-Shirts, but when moisture collects in your socks they may ruck up and cause blistering. Use socks of synthetic fibre which do not soak up moisture. One method of safeguarding against blisters is to wear two thin pairs of socks, although some socks are now made in two layers to give you this same effect.

Gizmos

There are only two technical gadgets which offer useful advantages for a runner. One is a wristwatch with a stopwatch function. Try to find one that has a large digital display. You may already have one of these. A lap/split function is also useful to record progress during a run. The second item is a heart-rate monitor. These were available long before they became robust and accurate enough to be very helpful. They are only beneficial, though, if you learn what they can tell you about the functioning of your body. An informed user can make sure that every effort is used to best effect in training. Above all, heart-rate monitors can warn when you are straining, and may later suffer for it.

When not to start

In some conditions, it's better not to run at all. Extreme cold or heat should be avoided. On hot summer days when the temperature rises above 25ºC (77ºF), it may be more comfortable to run earlier in the morning, when it is still cool. Alternatively, when roads and pavements are icy, or packed with hard snow, you risk falling. Even relatively slight slippage between your feet and the running surface can lead to tightening muscles and an increased likelihood of injury.

Useful Extras

You may find the additional items useful, depending on your own preferences and conditions.

HEART RATE MONITOR

USED KNOWLEDGEABLY, A HEART RATE MONITOR WILL HELP YOU GET THE MOST OUT OF YOUR TRAINING.

FLEECE HAT

ONLY NECESSARY IN VERY COLD CONDITIONS.

WINTER GLOVES

A THIN PAIR WILL BE SUFFICIENT TO PREVENT FINGERS NUMBING.

EAR WARMER

YOUR EARS MAY NEED PROTECTION FROM THE COLD EVEN WHEN A HAT FEELS TOO HOT.

CAP

THE PEAK WILL PROTECT YOUR FACE FROM DRIVING RAIN.

JACKET

YOU MAY NEED A WINDPROOF OUTER LAYER. TRY TO FIND ONE WHICH LETS YOUR SWEAT OUT, EITHER THROUGH THE FABRIC OR BY PARTLY UNZIPPING IT.

T-SHIRT

THE BASIC TRAINING ITEM, BUT IF YOU WEAR IT UNDERNEATH OUTER CLOTHING, GO FOR THE 'TECHNICAL' TYPE.

RACE SHOES

WEARING LIGHTER, LESS PROTECTIVE SHOES FOR RACING WILL ONLY BE WORTHWHILE FOR SOME PEOPLE.

SORBOTHANE HEEL PADS

THESE PROVIDE PROTECTION FROM IMPACT ON HARD RUNNING SURFACES.

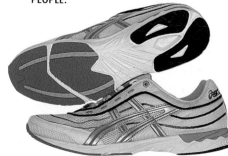

4
Building up endurance

Fitness is only a meaningful concept when applied to particular tasks. Your fitness to run a marathon depends mainly on your endurance. Building it up is the main task of any marathon training programme.

Assessing your fitness level

If your activity extends to more than running for the bus, you still need to assess your level of fitness with regards to running a marathon. You may cycle to work, swim or play football once or twice a week, but it's difficult to know how much this may contribute to a base for marathon running.

By far the best training for running is running itself. You may be able to simulate a running effect on the heart and lungs, but the exercise you choose to achieve this will probably exert very different muscle groups. Even when your existing activity incorporates quite a lot of running, as in a football match, it may be done under different conditions and in a different way to endurance running.

Footballers can often run fast – for short distances. Action on the pitch is all start-stop, which has far less of an impact on aerobic fitness than long, uninterrupted runs. As any runner who plays the occasional game of football can tell the following day, running in a match uses different muscles as you move backwards, sideways and diagonally more than you move forwards.

The key thing is not to make assumptions about what you can do, but gently test out your level of fitness – as it specifically applies to long-distance running (technically, "long-distance" can mean anything more than a mile).

The "landmark run" suggested at the beginning of the last chapter is as good a way as any to put yourself to the test (see page 25). Then you can adjust the length of this basic run in accordance with your reactions, but make sure that you rest at least one day before trying again. It may not be clear how your muscles have responded until 48 hours afterwards. If you still feel stiffness 48 hours later, postpone the next run for another day.

Stress and recovery

The basic principle of all training is to put

PRACTICE MAKES PERFECT: THE BEST TRAINING FOR RUNNING IS RUNNING ITSELF.

your body under stress, and then allow it to recover. Only after recovery will the training benefits start to build up, as the body adapts to the stress. If you do not allow adequate rest to recover from this stress, there will be no training benefit. Instead, you will wear yourself out and find that your performance deteriorates.

Even well-trained athletes may occasionally experience this "over-training" syndrome. It often occurs when the body requires more time to recover than normal. This might be because of other stresses in life, or because the body is suffering from some undetected ailment. When you start to run regularly

you don't know what time is "normal" for recovery. You are placing new stresses on your body and it takes time to assess how much recovery is required. It's always better to err on the side of caution to make sure you aren't accumulating fatigue from one training session to the next.

The first requirement in any training programme is to adapt to the stress/recovery cycle. You cannot do this in isolation from what else is happening

in your life. If you have taken on extra commitments recently – physical, mental, emotional – it may be better to postpone the start of a training programme until you have the time and energy available to accommodate it.

Don't let this become the excuse for indefinite postponement. You should only delay until such time as you have an established routine in place. Then, if you seriously want to start running, you will have to adapt your routine to make space for your training. This may require further adjustment of other activities, such as less socialising or replacing a commute to work with a run to work, or you may want to replace general fitness activities with time specifically spent running.

Basic training

The "landmark" run helps you gauge your level of fitness as it applies to running. Once you have adjusted your initial expectation to the reality of the effort, you will have one element in place. This is a bigger achievement than it sounds. You have identified the building block you require. You then have to assemble many of these blocks, fitting them together as snugly as possible. If at first you can only manage one of these runs every three days, then an immediate objective could be to increase the frequency to every other day.

This may not be appropriate for everyone. Other commitments may mean that it is difficult for you to run every other day, particularly at first when "doing a training session" is a novel and significant activity. If this is the case, try extending the distance of the run rather than the frequency. This is certainly more time-efficient, but be careful to avoid overextending yourself during any one outing. In the longer term it will be

necessary to increase both the frequency and the length of your runs, but it is much better to tackle things in the easiest possible way.

Avoid repetition, by selecting landmarks that take you in different directions from your home, and rotate your run among these alternative routes. It may be that one particular run is much more appealing than the others. If this is the case, and you prefer to repeat the same run each time, avoid making direct comparisons between the time you take to do the run from one day to the next.

In the long term, you will notice the difference. You will find it much easier to complete one specific run, and will naturally tend to quicken your pace slightly to complete it in less time. This is not something that is noticeable from one day to the next, but from week to week and month to month the training will take effect, and you should be able to run further and faster than you could before. If you doubt this, time yourself over one run. Do the same a month later. Your watch will show you that your performance has improved.

The priority at this stage is not to get quicker at doing the same basic run that you selected as your starter. You need to move on to more substantial fare. As you become comfortable with running one mile at a time, increase the length of every other run to 1½ miles (2km). Then make all your runs of this length. After a short while doing this, try tackling 2 miles (3km) every other run, and so on.

Don't set yourself quantified objectives in advance, like doubling your mileage each week. Increase the distance only when you feel that you have fully adapted to your existing workload. Increasing the distance that you can comfortably run in one session, and the frequency of your runs are the twin objectives at this stage. If you do want to reassure yourself with evidence of your improvement, then go back to the shorter run you were doing a month

FITNESS IS EVENT-SPECIFIC. THE START-STOP ACTION OF A FOOTBALL MATCH BUILDS UP ONLY LIMITED ENDURANCE CAPABILITIES.

RUNNING IN COMPANY CAN MAKE THE MILES GO BY MORE EASILY.

ago to see how much easier it feels and how much faster you can do it – without any increase in your normal level of effort.

Basic training, in running terms, may loosely be defined as running several miles or kilometres a day, several times a week. This could be 3 miles (4.5km) a day, twice a week – in which case it is very basic, or it could mean 5 miles (7.5km) a day four times a week – in which case it may be time to move on to a training programme specifically geared towards running a marathon.

Building endurance

If you are starting to train with the objective of running a marathon in mind, there are two issues to contend with. One is the requirement to run, the other is the sheer distance over which you have to sustain your effort. So far we have concentrated exclusively on starting to run, over very modest distances.

Over time, as the training takes effect, these distances can be extended. It was suggested that the first stumble into the unknown be towards a local landmark only 400m or yards away. After repeated, programmed efforts, a couple of months later you may be running

three miles every other day. The full marathon distance of 26.2 miles may still look like a very distant objective, even after all this hard work.

In fact, you have already made the most important step. You have become a regular runner. By now, running should have become a lot easier and a lot more enjoyable than it may have been. There is a straightforward path from where you are now to the ultimate objective of completing a marathon. That's not to say the path is short, but it does not involve any more difficult terrain than that which lies behind you.

Even so, it may be difficult to visualise how you will eventually be able to run two weeks' worth of your current mileage in just one run. If this prospect intimidates you, and undermines your confidence in completing a marathon, then you may need to try something different and approach the task from a different direction.

Running and walking

Walking could be the answer. It's less tiring than running, and you can keep going longer. Walking a marathon is less daunting a prospect than running one, except that it would take about nine hours to complete it. Walking for long distances is a good way of becoming used to being active for long periods. You

may take five hours or more to complete your first marathon, and walking for that length of time prepares you in a different way to running for a shorter time.

Compared to previous experience, you will be building endurance by running for half an hour. Walking for half a day – or as long as you expect it would take you to cover the marathon distance – cultivates your persistence more than your endurance. There is a fine line between the two, and you will need both to see you through your first marathon. It is worthwhile spending long periods on your feet, moving, at the same time as you are getting used to running increasingly longer – but at the moment still not very long – distances.

These experiences should converge towards each other. Most marathon runners do a long run once a week, considerably further than a normal day's training. The easiest way for a beginner to do this is to mix running with walking on the "long runs", at the same time as the normal run is increasing in length. If you can handle half an hour of running as a normal run, once a week it is worth alternating 15 minutes of running with 15 minutes of walking for an hour. You may find that the periods of walking allow you to recover sufficiently so that you can manage 90 minutes of run/walk.

Although mixing running with walking will extend the time and distance of your longest outings, it probably won't yet approach the time required to cover a marathon. However, you should approach this target distance, or time, much more quickly with a run/walk session. This should give you the encouragement you need to keep focusing on the ultimate task which otherwise might still seem too distant to provide much motivational force.

STEP RIGHT UP: RUNNERS IN THE GREAT WALL MARATHON IN CHINA FACE UNIQUE ENDURANCE PROBLEMS.

5
Warming Up

You can start your run as soon as you leave home, but leaping abruptly into action can cause damage. Guard against injury by following a few simple preliminaries.

A great advantage to taking up running as a sport is that there is very little wasted time. What you do counts, from the moment you step outside your front door. No need to waste time getting into a car and driving to a particular venue. The world is at your feet, and you can convert any part of it into a training venue simply by breaking into a run.

This was what was suggested as a way of getting started. You do not have to think about training as anything more intimidating than running for a bus. The landmark run which got you started was devised to involve minimum fuss and disruption to normal routine. But once you are committed to running as a long-term pursuit, it is worth performing certain rituals in order to prevent your new adventure grinding to a premature halt.

When you run, you suddenly impose greater demands on your system than those it is used to coping with at walking pace. You breathe deeper and quicker, your heart beats more, your muscles contract more rapidly and your joints have to accommodate greater jarring.

Your body is capable of responding to these demands, but it may need a little coaxing to do so. Gradually increasing the workload involved in any training session is one aspect that was discussed in the previous chapter (see page 34). Overlaid on this progression, over weeks and months, is the daily cycle within which your training has to find its place.

Body rhythm

Your body gradually "warms up" during the day, so that exercise can be performed more easily in the afternoon or evening. During the Olympics heats are held in the morning, but finals are always in the evening. Although this is much to do with public viewing habits, the increasing demands of the competitive schedule correspond to

the daily internal rhythm of the athlete's body.

When you wake up from a night's sleep, you are at a particularly low ebb. For the last several hours your body has been, if not quite switched off, then literally dormant. It is expecting a lot to go from this state of bodily bewilderment to exerting yourself to any significant extent.

For most people, running first thing in the morning is by far the most

NIGHT FINALS MATCH THE BODY'S RHYTHM: PAULA RADCLIFFE WINNING THE EUROPEAN 10,000M CHAMPIONSHIP IN RECO.

convenient arrangement. Work life takes over from 09.00. There is no guarantee that it will leave you with enough energy and resolve to fit in a run at the end of the day. By that time your new ambitions may crumble before the everyday reality. To avoid this, you need to create circumstances such that running home from work is not voluntary, but something demanded of you. Otherwise, resign yourself to an early morning effort.

World-class athletes train twice daily – maybe even three times. The function of the first training session of the day is to warm the body up to the tasks it will face later in a more arduous training session. It is asking far too much to emulate this example in full, but you can do so in miniature.

Before any training session (or any race) a warm-up can prepare your body for the demands that will be placed upon it. To prime your body systems for these tasks, two things are required. Firstly, you need to raise your pulse rate and the consequent delivery of oxygen to your muscles and, secondly, you need to stretch your muscles so that they have enough flexibility to accommodate the action of running.

Muscles are more flexible when primed with a good blood supply, or "warmed up", so stretching should come after a certain amount of exercise. Five minutes of gentle jogging would be a good warm-up for a stretching routine. If you do this warm-up as the first part of your run, before stopping to stretch, you may find yourself a little exposed.

In summer, if you can get as far as a local park, you may find it warm enough to stretch there. It's also probably the only public place where you can stretch without embarrassment. Many people do this, particularly early in the morning on before-work runs. There are usually some convenient props to use, too: for example, trees to lean against and waste bins or seats to rest your leg upon.

In the winter, it's just too cold to do stationary exercises outdoors. By the time you finished your routine your bones would be chilled rather than your muscles warmed up. You can still do a stretching routine after a warm-up, if you first run a short circuit around the local area – a few blocks – and return home to stretch before departing again on the main part of your run. This may strike you as a bit overelaborate and, once you have got out of the front door, it may seem a better idea not to come back through it until the planned run is completed.

A treadmill would solve the problem, but is expensive, space-consuming and noisy. It is almost as effective simply to run on the spot. In fact, to avoid jarring it may be better to walk on the spot, but using a high knee-lift, pointing the toes and exaggerating your arm swing. This at least eases your body into action and gets some blood flowing into the muscles after their long night of inactivity. Walking up and down the stairs a few times would also do the trick.

Stretching

Once you have roused yourself in this way, you should do a few stretching exercises. They need not be elaborate – just a few stretches on each leg, one for each of the main muscles you use during running. Runners are often dismissive of stretching, regarding it as time which could be better spent on the run. Try to separate the two activities so that you do not think of doing one at the expense of the other. Set aside five minutes at the beginning and the end of the run to do a few simple stretches. By doing this you will greatly reduce the risk of sustaining muscular injuries.

Running is a repetitive exercise which tightens the muscle fibres. This tightening, if not counterbalanced by some other activity, shortens the muscle and leads to a significant loss of flexibility. Flexibility of the muscles – the extra "play" they have beyond that required for the basic repetitive task of putting one foot in front of the other – is an insurance against injury. Stretching is the means to maintain flexibility.

Stretching should be gradual, towards the particular muscle's natural limit of extension. You will feel resistance from the muscle when you begin to approach this limit. Stop there, and hold the position for 30 seconds or so. Do not "bounce", or in any way force the muscle to extend further. Like running capabilities, flexibility improves with regular repetition of the exercise. Overstretching – pursuing a stretch to a point where you experience discomfort – leads directly to injury.

Before starting to stretch, find a place where you can do so without being disturbed by other people in the house brushing past you. The hamstring stretch involves using some furniture, such as stairs or a chair, to provide a surface for resting the leg you are stretching. You may also find that a cushion under your heel offers greater comfort for this stretch.

Muscles operate in "antagonistic" pairs, alternately contracting against each other. You should take care to stretch both sets of muscles, rather than letting one become more flexible and out of balance with its "antagonistic" other. If this happens, the risk of injury increases.

The muscles which do most work when you are running are the hamstrings, down the back of your thigh, the quadriceps down the front, and the calf muscles, the soleus and the gastrocnemus. At the very least you need to stretch each of these muscles in turn. The following exercises will allow you to do this...

TRAINING NOT STRAINING: RUNNING WITH A PARTNER REQUIRES A CERTAIN PHYSICAL AND MENTAL COMPATIBILITY.

Quadriceps stretch

Stand on your right leg, while steadying yourself with your right hand perhaps against a wall, or holding on to a piece of furniture. Reach behind you with your left hand and grasp your left foot just above your toes. Pull the foot directly back (not to one side or the other), so that the left heel touches the left buttock, or comes as close to this position as possible without causing discomfort. You will feel the stretch in the quadriceps muscle at the front of the thigh. Hold this position for 30 seconds and then release, slowly returning the foot to the ground. Repeat the exercise while standing on your left leg to stretch the quadriceps muscle of the right leg.

Hamstring stretch (standing)

Stand with your feet together in front of a level, raised surface. This could be at the bottom of a staircase, or a short distance in front of a chair or settee back. Extend one leg, keeping it locked straight, and rest it on the surface at a height of your choosing. This should not be so high that it causes you discomfort. Relax your leg muscles and keep the vertebrae of your lower back locked in a straight position. Then slowly bend your trunk forward, keeping the lower back vertebrae locked. As you lean your trunk forward you will feel the stretch at the back of your thigh, in the hamstring muscle. Once you feel this, hold the stretch in that position for 30 seconds and then gradually straighten your trunk and bring your leg back to the ground. Repeat the exercise with your other leg.

Hamstring stretch (sitting)

Sit on the floor with one leg extended and the other bent out to the side and your arms at your sides. Keep your trunk vertical and lock the vertebrae of the lower back. Relax your leg muscles and slowly bend your trunk forward, keeping the lower back vertebrae locked. As you lean forward, you will feel the stretch at the back of your thigh, in the hamstring muscle. Once you feel this, hold the stretch in that position for 30 seconds and then gradually straighten your trunk. Repeat the exercise with your other leg.

Calf stretch (1)

Stand in front of a level surface of about waist height, such as stairs, a counter or a windowsill. A vertical wall will also serve. Lean against this object, keeping one foot flat on the floor and the leg straight, locked at the knee. Allow your other leg to relax, with the foot merely resting lightly on the ground in case you need to steady yourself. Use your arms to vary the angle the stretched leg makes with the floor, or adjust your distance from the object to do this. As the angle becomes more acute, you will begin to feel the stretch in the upper part of the calf, just below the knee joint. Hold the position for 30 seconds, and then gradually relax by transferring your body weight on to the other foot. Repeat the exercise using the other leg.

Gluteal stretch

Sit on the floor and draw one leg towards you with the foot flat on the floor and hooked over the other leg, and the knee pointing upwards. Draw your foot as close to your body as is comfortable, until you feel the stretch in your buttock.

Clasp your arms around your knee and gently pull it towards you, almost making contact with your chin – but do not dip your head. Maintain the stretch for 30 seconds.

Relax and repeat with the other leg.

Calf stretch (2)

Stand in front of a vertical surface, like a wall or door frame, about a metre or yard away from it. Lean forward slightly, with your hands against the wall or door jamb. Extend one leg forward, with the foot flat on the ground quite close to your vertical surface. Keep the other foot flat on the floor. Bend this leg at the knee, so that it lowers both towards the wall and the ground while bearing your body weight.

Your other leg should be relaxed, also bent at the knee, but bearing only its own weight. Your hands against the wall, in this exercise, only fulfil the steadying function. As the angle between your lower leg and the floor becomes more acute you will begin to feel the stretch in the lower part of the calf, where it connects to the Achilles tendon. Hold the position for 30 seconds and then gradually relax by transferring your body weight on to the other foot. Repeat the exercise using the other leg.

Groin stretch

Sit on the floor, put your hands around your ankles and draw your feet towards you – so that the soles are touching each other and the knees are pointing outwards and slightly upward. With your hands still clasped around your ankles, rest your your forearms against the insides of your legs, just above the knee. Gently press down with your forearms so that your knees lower slightly towards the floor. You will feel the stretch in your groin. Do not force it. Maintain the stretch for 30 seconds. Rest and repeat.

6
Training Diary

To start running, motivation is the key. Starting to train for a particular marathon ties you down to setting yourself specific tasks and goals as stepping stones in your preparation.

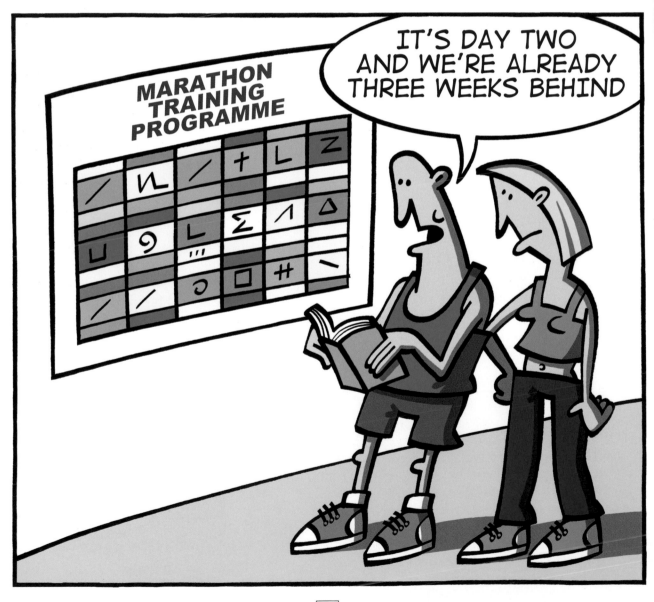

The training programme which follows lasts 16 weeks, from the moment you embark upon it through to marathon day. This in itself should crystallise any of the doubts you may have had. All speculation "Can I do it?" must now be automatically answered by mental resolve "Yes I can".

Only two ingredients are absolutely essential to the programme: regular sessions during the week – four or five times per week, and one long training session to develop endurance. Speed training is another aspect you may wish to introduce, but it is a refinement.

By default there is a third key element: rest. You must space out the effort within the training programme so that you can recover adequately between runs. Recovery can often be assisted by exercising differently. Swimming, cycling and walking will all complement your running programme. Use the training log to record all the exercise you undertake during the 16 weeks, not just the running.

Massage is another means by which you can assist recovery. Sports massagists have multiplied over the last decade, and many of them have a background in running. Apart from being a method of injury treatment, massage can assist recovery and act as an early warning system against injury. It will alert you to stresses and imbalances that may be building up in your muscles, and help to diffuse them. For a list of qualified practitioners consult the therapists' directory at www.lssm.com.

The training programme outlined is not a blueprint to be imposed upon your life, redesigning your existence. It is a set of suggestions, the practicality and usefulness of which will vary according to your personal circumstances. Weekday running is best fitted into your daily routine with minimum disruption to it.

Many people prefer to do their run early in the morning, to "get it out of the way". This is not necessarily the best

KEEPING REGULAR: ARRANGING TO RUN WITH SOMEONE HELPS KEEP A ROUTINE.

time to subject your body to it, but it does mean less chance of backsliding in the face of work pressures. At the end of the day you may not feel up to it. If a midday break is long enough, this may be a good time to run, as long as you do not skip lunch afterwards.

How you fit in the training is still to be resolved, but on entering this "countdown" phase you should be confidently running for half an hour every other day, with one of these being a longer session. Which days you run is a matter of personal choice, as long as they are interspersed with enough time to recover.

Alternative approaches to the key endurance session have already been outlined. Week by week you can gradually increase the distance (or time) you run, or you can start off by combining running and walking in your long training session and gradually increase the proportion of running.

Races can be used as an incentive to complete particular target distances, and as a means of familiarising yourself with race conditions. This would include developing a pre-race routine for eating, drinking, using what toilet facilities may be available, and coping with crowded starts (see page 108, "Marathon Week"). None of this is particularly complicated,

but familiarity may increase the ease with which you approach a race.

One of the weekday training sessions increases in significance during the 16-week programme. At first the programme calls for it to be lengthened, and halfway towards the marathon date more varied running is recommended. This introduces you to running faster, or at least with greater effort for short periods within the overall run. The effort can be varied according to terrain, and this is recommended as a first step towards "speed training". Running strongly up hills helps to develop a feel for the demands of "speedwork" which you may want to pursue through the sort of "fartlek" session described in week 8 (9 weeks to go).

Weeks 5, 9 and 12 incorporate the opportunity to rest more than in the other weeks. This is to allow your body to better absorb the efforts of the intervening weeks during which you have been increasing your workload, and approach the next block of training with renewed vigour. On the same basis, the last two weeks – and especially the last week – will consist of relatively little running, to allow your body to rest adequately before the marathon.

There are other aspects affecting your ability to complete the marathon which must be attended to in this final week. These are the subject of the final Marathon Week (page 106).

Things are unlikely to go so smoothly that you can follow all the recommendations as laid out here. During the 16 weeks you may well pick up a cold, or some kind of injury. You may find that you are unable to devote as much time to running as you had hoped. There are all sorts of reasons why you may have to depart from the training programme, and there are plenty of other problems which you may encounter. Refer to Chapter 8 "Common Problems" for suggestions about how you might cope with unexpected circumstances.

WEEK 1

SUNDAY

16 weeks to go

Running four times a week, as recommended here, means that you will be doing two sessions on consecutive days of the week. For most people the days most appropriate for this would be Saturday and Sunday. Not only are you then not restricted to times before or after work, but you will probably have more time to relax in between runs, from one day to the next. Beware though, that if you have a heavy Saturday night out it may be counter-productive to cut short your sleep on Sunday morning in order to run off your indulgence of the night before.

Most people choose Sunday morning for their longer run of the week, and most races are held then, too. The suggested programme is based on the assumption of (relatively) free weekends, but if your week is ordered differently, then your training will have to be likewise.

The other two runs are spread out during the week, one on Tuesday and one on Thursday, with rest days in between. It may be that you prefer to run on other days, but make sure that you have regularly-spaced rest days. It is a question of fitting in the recovery as much as it is of fitting in the running. Be especially careful to allow a recovery day after your long run.

WEEK 1

Suggested Routine

SUNDAY	Longer run – one hour, walking for short periods if necessary
MONDAY	recovery
TUESDAY	30 minutes running
WEDNESDAY	recovery
THURSDAY	30 minutes running
FRIDAY	recovery
SATURDAY	30 minutes running

Thought for the Day:
You have brains in your head, you have feet in your shoes.
You can steer yourself in any direction you choose
– Dr Seuss

STATISTICS

Date:

Time of day: AM/PM

Conditions:

Location:

Estimated distance: miles   kilometers

Time (duration):   hrs   mins

Aims:
....
....
....
....

TRAINING TIP
If you can't find a training partner to run with, try getting someone to ride alongside you. The simple fact of having company concentrates the mind and makes the miles pass more easily.

Warm-up:

Warm-down:

Other exercise today:

Run details:
....
....
....
....
....

Accompanied by:

Comments:
....
....
....
....

MONDAY

Thought for the Day:
Fall down seven times, stand up eight times
– Japanese proverb

STATISTICS

Date:

Time of day: AM/PM

Conditions:

Location:

Estimated distance: miles kilometers

Time (duration): hrs mins

Aims:

TRAINING TIP

Even on rest days you can exercise. Doing the pre-run stretches, whether or not you run that day, helps both to maintain flexibility and to reinforce the routine you need to create for your running.

Warm-up:

Warm-down:

Other exercise today:

Run details:

Accompanied by:

Comments:

TUESDAY

Thought for the Day:
Happiness is a state of activity
– Aristotle

STATISTICS

Date:

Time of day: AM/PM

Conditions:

Location:

Estimated distance: miles kilometers

Time (duration): hrs mins

Aims:

TRAINING TIP

Are your shoelaces secure? Tie them in a double bow, and tuck the ends under the lacing to prevent them flapping around and working themselves loose as you run.

Warm-up:

Warm-down:

Other exercise today:

Run details:

Accompanied by:

Comments:

WEEK 1

WEDNESDAY

Thought for the Day:
It takes seventy-two muscles to frown, but only thirteen to smile
– Anon

STATISTICS

Date:
Time of day: AM/PM
Conditions:

Location:
Estimated distance: miles   kilometers
Time (duration): hrs   mins

Aims:

TRAINING TIP
To reinforce the running habit, try thinking about running even on your rest days. Would you be able to fit in a run if you wanted to? How long would you run and where would you go?

Warm-up:
Warm-down:
Other exercise today:

Run details:

Accompanied by:

Comments:

THURSDAY

Thought for the Day:
Either you run the day, or the day runs you
– Jim Rohn

STATISTICS

Date:
Time of day: AM/PM
Conditions:

Location:
Estimated distance: miles   kilometers
Time (duration): hrs   mins

Aims:

TRAINING TIP
When you feel aches and pains, don't battle against them. Evaluate how they feel as you go along. Slow down, but try to decide if they result from normal tiredness or muscle stiffness, or whether they may be the first signs of something more serious,.

Warm-up:
Warm-down:
Other exercise today:

Run details:

Accompanied by:

Comments:

FRIDAY

Thought for the Day:
Your thoughts are the architects of your destiny
– David O McKay

STATISTICS

Date:

Time of day: AM/PM

Conditions:

Location:

Estimated distance: miles   kilometers

Time (duration):   hrs   mins

Aims:

TRAINING TIP

You may not know just how your muscles are taking the new routine. Book a massage early on in your training, and the masseur will be able to assess your muscular condition – if the experience of the massage doesn't indicate this to you directly.

Warm-up:

Warm-down:

Other exercise today:

Run details:

Accompanied by:

Comments:

SATURDAY

Thought for the Day:
Great changes may not happen right away, but with effort even the difficult may become easy
– Bill Blackman

STATISTICS

Date:

Time of day: AM/PM

Conditions:

Location:

Estimated distance: miles   kilometers

Time (duration):   hrs   mins

Aims:

TRAINING TIP

Experiment with what you eat before you run. You may find you feel better running after eating something, rather than on an empty stomach – especially if you run first thing in the morning.

Warm-up:

Warm-down:

Other exercise today:

Run details:

Accompanied by:

Comments:

WEEK 1

WEEK 2

SUNDAY

15 weeks to go

There was nothing in last week's training that should have been unduly taxing, but you may have found it difficult to sustain your run for a full hour.

Running in company can help. With someone else alongside you have other things to think of than your own discomfort, and whether this is sufficient reason to stop. Conversation can make time pass, and the miles, without feeling the effort so much.

The ultimate in running in company is to run in a race. You may feel this is too much to cope with as yet, but it can be a way of familiarising yourself with the experience to which your training is ultimately directed. You should look only for a 10km race, and a low-key one at that. Around Christmas and New Year there are several 'Turkey Trot' or 'Christmas Pud' runs which might be appropriate.

Beware the tendency to run significantly faster in races. Make sure you warm up with a mile of easy jogging, and then start the race modestly, no faster than your training pace. Your effort should be directed towards maintaining this pace for the full 10km without any break rather than anything more ambitious. Make sure you do another slow jog for a mile to warm down, then some of the stretching exercises.

If you are drawn into running significantly faster than normal, your legs will be stiff over the next couple of days. You may need to extend your recovery over two days, and only resume running on the Wednesday.

Weekday runs should be lengthened slightly but don't do this if you are suffering from your earlier exertions.

Suggested Routine

SUNDAY	Longer run – one hour, trying to avoid walking or 10km race at training pace
MONDAY	recovery
TUESDAY	35 minutes running
WEDNESDAY	recovery
THURSDAY	35 minutes running
FRIDAY	recovery
SATURDAY	30 minutes running

Thought for the Day:
Wheresoever you go, go with all your heart
– Confucius

STATISTICS

Date:

Time of day: AM/PM

Conditions:

Location:

Estimated distance: miles   kilometers

Time (duration):   hrs   mins

Aims:

TRAINING TIP

Start your longer runs or your races slowly. If you have energy to spare later on in the run it will allow you to more than recoup any possible losses you may suffer from starting slowly.

Warm-up:

Warm-down:

Other exercise today:

Run details:

Accompanied by:

Comments:

WEEK 2

MONDAY	TUESDAY

Thought for the Day:
If I work toward an end, meantime I am confined to a process
– Hugh Prather

Thought for the Day:
Discipline is the bridge between goals and accomplishment
– Jim Rohn

STATISTICS

Date:
Time of day: AM/PM
Conditions:

Location:
Estimated distance: miles kilometers
Time (duration): hrs mins

Aims:

STATISTICS

Date:
Time of day: AM/PM
Conditions:

Location:
Estimated distance: miles kilometers
Time (duration): hrs mins

Aims:

TRAINING TIP

Try to assess your recovery from the longer runs. How do you feel the following day, and the day after that? If you are finding it hard to run two days later, you may need to change the pattern of your training to accommodate this.

TRAINING TIP

Drink a glass or two of water a short while before you run. In the morning you will be slightly dehydrated from the moisture you have sweated out overnight. Your run will be more comfortable if you restore the balance.

Warm-up:
Warm-down:
Other exercise today:

Run details:

Accompanied by:

Comments:

Warm-up:
Warm-down:
Other exercise today:

Run details:

Accompanied by:

Comments:

WEEK 2

WEDNESDAY	THURSDAY

Thought for the Day:
Be thou the rainbow in the storms of life
– Lord Byron

Thought for the Day:
Happiness is not a station you arrive at, but a manner of travelling
– Margaret B Runbeck

STATISTICS

STATISTICS

Date:

Time of day: AM/PM

Conditions:

Location:

Estimated distance: miles   kilometers

Time (duration): hrs   mins

Aims:

Date:

Time of day: AM/PM

Conditions:

Location:

Estimated distance: miles   kilometers

Time (duration): hrs   mins

Aims:

TRAINING TIP

Find out what energy drink may be offered in the marathon which you intend to run. Try it on a rest day. The first test is palatability. If you can't stomach it at rest, it's unlikely you will be able to take it during the race.

TRAINING TIP

Check the weather before you run. You will register if it is raining, but if you run early in the morning it easy to misjudge the temperature. Simply opening the front door before stepping outside will allow you to ascertain how much clothing you need.

Warm-up:

Warm-down:

Other exercise today:

Run details:

Accompanied by:

Comments:

Warm-up:

Warm-down:

Other exercise today:

Run details:

Accompanied by:

Comments:

WEEK 2

FRIDAY	**SATURDAY**

Thought for the Day:
Do not let your fears choose your destiny
– anon

Thought for the Day:
Ever tried. Ever failed. No matter. Try again, fail again, fail better
– Samuel Beckett

STATISTICS

Date:

Time of day: AM/PM

Conditions:

Location:

Estimated distance: miles   kilometers

Time (duration):   hrs   mins

Aims:

STATISTICS

Date:

Time of day: AM/PM

Conditions:

Location:

Estimated distance: miles   kilometers

Time (duration):   hrs   mins

Aims:

TRAINING TIP

Pay attention to food labelling. Check the carbohydrate/sugar and fat/saturated fat content of foods. Try to avoid sugary foods and saturated fat. You may need sugary food immediately after running but at other times it will distort the regularity of eating at mealtimes.

TRAINING TIP

Check the wear on your shoes. if you have only been wearing one pair you may have worn them down so they exacerbate any irregularities of your running gait. If you can see obvious signs of wear on the heel you may need to get a different pair.

Warm-up:

Warm-down:

Other exercise today:

Run details:

Accompanied by:

Comments:

Warm-up:

Warm-down:

Other exercise today:

Run details:

Accompanied by:

Comments:

WEEK 3

SUNDAY

14 weeks to go

Continue to increase the time you spend running, both in the long run and in the other sessions. Lengthen the long run steadily, so that it does not cause you strain, over the first 10 weeks of the 16-week preparation period. Then you consolidate, but the earlier you can get used to running for extended periods without walking, the better equipped you will be for tackling the rest of the programme.

This week, aim is to run for 90 minutes. Take walking breaks if you need to do so in order to keep going. The increase in time on your feet is significant, and you may not be able to judge it correctly at first. Try not to strain in order to complete the full 90 minutes. If you exert yourself too much it will affect your ability to complete the rest of the training.

Increase the duration of the other runs while maintaining the pace. The body takes some time to prime itself at the start of a run. You may spend 15 minutes of each run just reaching an optimum level of performance. Then you will need to spend the final five minutes of a run gently easing your pace down. This means that you may be at your maximum workrate for only 10 minutes of a half-hour run.

Your regular run has increased by 10 minutes. This may not seem a lot, although it may feel it. Increasing the run to 40 minutes can double the duration of its most productive phase.

Suggested Routine

SUNDAY	Longer run or run/walk for 90 minutes
MONDAY	recovery
TUESDAY	40 minutes running
WEDNESDAY	recovery
THURSDAY	40 minutes running
FRIDAY	recovery
SATURDAY	40 minutes running

Thought for the Day:
There's a long, long rail a-winding
Into the land of my dreams
– Stoddard King

STATISTICS

Date:

Time of day: AM/PM

Conditions:

Location:

Estimated distance: miles   kilometres

Time (duration):   hrs   mins

Aims:

TRAINING TIP

Shoes get great attention, but socks are rarely noticed. Check yours to see if they are threadbare. If you poke holes in the toes during a run you will end up with blisters

Warm-up:

Warm-down:

Other exercise today:

Run details:

Accompanied by:

Comments:

MONDAY

Thought for the Day:
When we quiet the mind, the symphony begins
– Anon

STATISTICS

Date:
Time of day: AM/PM
Conditions:

Location:
Estimated distance: miles   kilometres
Time (duration): hrs   mins

Aims:

TRAINING TIP

To assist recovery from training try to schedule some quiet time as a reward for the previous day's efforts. Put your feet up and watch a film once in a while.

Warm-up:
Warm-down:
Other exercise today:

Run details:

Accompanied by:

Comments:

TUESDAY

Thought for the Day:
People who like this sort of thing will find this the sort of thing they like
– Abraham Lincoln

STATISTICS

Date:
Time of day: AM/PM
Conditions:

Location:
Estimated distance: miles   kilometres
Time (duration): hrs   mins

Aims:

TRAINING TIP

If you ever get the chance to run unobstructed in a race, make sure you cut from corner to corner and do not stick to the same side of the road. The race is measured this way, and you do not need to add gratuitous distance on.

Warm-up:
Warm-down:
Other exercise today:

Run details:

Accompanied by:

Comments:

WEEK 3

WEDNESDAY

Thought for the Day:
Festina lente ("hasten slowly")
– Suetonis

STATISTICS

Date:

Time of day: AM/PM

Conditions:

Location:

Estimated distance: miles kilometres

Time (duration): hrs mins

Aims:

TRAINING TIP

Is there anything you can do to make it easier out the door in the morning? Elastic shoelaces are used by triathletes to reduce the time they spend in the transition area. They may also save the crucial minute that allows you to get to work on time.

Warm-up:

Warm-down:

Other exercise today:

Run details:

Accompanied by:

Comments:

THURSDAY

Thought for the Day:
Yes, sir, puffing is of various sorts; the principal are the puff direct, the puff preliminary, the puff collateral, and the puff oblique, or puff by implication – Richard Brinsley Sheridan, *The Critic*

STATISTICS

Date:

Time of day: AM/PM

Conditions:

Location:

Estimated distance: miles kilometres

Time (duration): hrs mins

Aims:

TRAINING TIP

If stitches trouble you, try to consciously move your diaphragm down to draw in a deep breath, and move it up to expel the air. If such deliberate deep breathing slows you, don't worry. You may be able to avoid grinding to a halt doing this.

Warm-up:

Warm-down:

Other exercise today:

Run details:

Accompanied by:

Comments:

WEEK 3

FRIDAY

Thought for the Day:
Fair is foul, and foul is fair; hover through the fog and filthy air
– Shakespeare, *Macbeth*

STATISTICS

Date:

Time of day: AM/PM

Conditions:

Location:

Estimated distance: miles   kilometres

Time (duration):   hrs   mins

Aims:

TRAINING TIP

Make sure you keep your toenails clipped. Be especially careful to ensure they are cut before you run any race. If not then you risk them being blackened by jarring against the end of the shoe, and dropping off over the next few months.

Warm-up:

Warm-down:

Other exercise today:

Run details:

Accompanied by:

Comments:

SATURDAY

Thought for the Day:
If exercise could be packed in a pill, it would be the single most widely prescribed and beneficial medecine
– US institute on Ageing

STATISTICS

Date:

Time of day: AM/PM

Conditions:

Location:

Estimated distance: miles   kilometres

Time (duration):   hrs   mins

Aims:

TRAINING TIP

If you are going to do the 10km race tomorrow, make this run an exercise in conserving energy. Run easily, and concentrate on feeling good. In a marathon this will be the main objective until well past the halfway mark.

Warm-up:

Warm-down:

Other exercise today:

Run details:

Accompanied by:

Comments:

WEEK 3

WEEK 4

SUNDAY

13 weeks to go

The long run should now be a consistently paced 90 minutes. If you prefer to run in a race, stick to a 10km but increase the length of your warm up and warm down. Warm up for 15 minutes. Try to extend your warm down to 20-30 minutes. Remember, these races are not ends in themselves, they are stepping stones towards your major goal of completing the marathon.

This week introduces another day's training. During the middle of the week you will be running for three days in a row. It is not as difficult as it may sound, as long as you can make the time for it. In terms of effort you can accommodate this extra session by reducing the length of the runs on Tuesday and Thursday. Eventually you will extend the midweek run into the number two session of the week.

By running three days in a row your body will need to adjust to "active recovery", in which you do not rest completely. Make sure you do not put too much effort into the days before or after a more intensive training day.

WEEK 4

Suggested Routine

SUNDAY	90 mins run, trying to avoid walking or 10km race with warm up and extended warm down
MONDAY	recovery
TUESDAY	30 minutes running
WEDNESDAY	30 minutes running
THURSDAY	30 minutes running
FRIDAY	recovery
SATURDAY	30 minutes running

Thought for the Day:
Twenty years from now you will be more disappointed by the things you didn't do than the things you did
– Mark Twain

STATISTICS

Date:

Time of day: AM/PM

Conditions:

Location:

Estimated distance: miles   kilometres

Time (duration): hrs   mins

Aims:

TRAINING TIP

If you want to simulate a crowded marathon start in a relatively small race, just line up at the back. This will make you start slower and gradually pick up your pace. In doing so, resist the temptation to dodge through the crowds at a too early stage.

Warm-up:

Warm-down:

Other exercise today:

Run details:

Accompanied by:

Comments:

MONDAY

Thought for the Day:
The less effort, the faster and more powerful you will be
– Bruce Lee

STATISTICS

Date:

Time of day: AM/PM

Conditions:

Location:

Estimated distance: miles   kilometres

Time (duration):   hrs   mins

Aims:

TRAINING TIP

Learn from experience. Whenever you run a race, analyse what you could do differently next time to improve the experience. This may be something you could do during a race, but is more likely to be something which you need to do before lining up at the start.

Warm-up:

Warm-down:

Other exercise today:

Run details:

Accompanied by:

Comments:

TUESDAY

Thought for the Day:
Today was good, today was fun.
Tomorrow is another one
– Dr Seuss

STATISTICS

Date:

Time of day: AM/PM

Conditions:

Location:

Estimated distance: miles   kilometres

Time (duration):   hrs   mins

Aims:

TRAINING TIP

If you run when it is still or already dark you should still stick to parks. You won't be able to get inside them, but running round the surrounding area will give you a much bigger block, with no cross streets to interrupt your flow.

Warm-up:

Warm-down:

Other exercise today:

Run details:

Accompanied by:

Comments:

WEEK 4

WEDNESDAY

Thought for the Day:
If you are doing your best, you will not have to worry about failure
– Robert Hillyer

STATISTICS

Date:

Time of day: AM/PM

Conditions:

Location:

Estimated distance: miles kilometres

Time (duration): hrs mins

Aims:

TRAINING TIP
If you have trouble tackling a complete run, break it down into parts and tackle each one as a separate objective in itself: to get up the big hill without slowing; to complete the next lap with least effort; or to gently ease up over the last mile.

Warm-up:

Warm-down:

Other exercise today:

Run details:

Accompanied by:

Comments:

THURSDAY

Thought for the Day:
The way was long, the wind was cold
– Sir Walter Scott

STATISTICS

Date:

Time of day: AM/PM

Conditions:

Location:

Estimated distance: miles kilometres

Time (duration): hrs mins

Aims:

TRAINING TIP
As your running gets more regular, perhaps related early morning needs do so as well. Check which public toilets are open along the route you run, and take your own supply of toilet paper

Warm-up:

Warm-down:

Other exercise today:

Run details:

Accompanied by:

Comments:

WEEK 4

FRIDAY

Thought for the Day:
The aim of life is to live, and to live is to be aware
– Henry Miller

STATISTICS

Date:

Time of day: AM/PM

Conditions:

Location:

Estimated distance: miles kilometres

Time (duration): hrs mins

Aims:

TRAINING TIP

Are you running in the best place? You may have started to do fixed routes over shorter distances. Now that you are going further, there may be better venues within range. in any case, keep your routes varied to maintain interest.

Warm-up:

Warm-down:

Other exercise today:

Run details:

Accompanied by:

Comments:

SATURDAY

Thought for the Day:
The real voyage of discovery consists not in seeking new landscapes, but in seeing with new eyes
– Marcel Proust

STATISTICS

Date:

Time of day: AM/PM

Conditions:

Location:

Estimated distance: miles kilometres

Time (duration): hrs mins

Aims:

TRAINING TIP

If you have got used to the taste of energy drink while at rest, the next test is to take it on the run. Stash a bottle somewhere on a loop course and take a swig each lap. You will need to repeat this exercise regularly, and rehearse it again just before the marathon.

Warm-up:

Warm-down:

Other exercise today:

Run details:

Accompanied by:

Comments:

WEEK 4

WEEK 5

12 weeks to go

There is a pattern to your training. You get used to doing something, and feel comfortable and confident with it, then the stakes are upped once more. This is fulfilling the purpose of training – that is, equipping you to tackle more taxing tasks, the ultimate of which is the marathon itself.

The task for this week is to further increase the length of your long run. You should be able to run for an unbroken 90 minutes, but you must continue to push against your limits. A two-hour run is a major achievement. If you can do this without breaks you are well advanced. If not, don't worry – take breaks when necessary.

It may be particularly helpful to walk up the hills. The heart rate goes up rapidly when you are climbing hills. On such

ascents you may exceed the level of effort your body can cope with without digging into your energy reserves. A heart rate monitor is useful for this. It can be set to sound when you exceed a particular heartbeat, warning you to back off. That is certainly the time to take a walking break. By doing this you will be making it easier for yourself to cope with longer periods on your feet at a consistent level of controlled effort.

Apart from lengthening the long run there is no other burden. The rest of the week is for recovery. Omit the Wednesday session if tired. Use this week to evaluate your recovery, Could you handle the training better if it was arranged differently within your week?

Suggested Routine

SUNDAY	Longer run – 90 minutes, or 2 hours run/walk
MONDAY	recovery
TUESDAY	30 minutes running
WEDNESDAY	30 minutes running
THURSDAY	30 minutes running
FRIDAY	recovery
SATURDAY	recovery

SUNDAY

Thought for the Day:
The end justifies the means
– Proverb, 17th century

STATISTICS

Date:

Time of day: AM/PM

Conditions:

Location:

Estimated distance: miles kilometres

Time (duration): hrs mins

Aims:

TRAINING TIP

On long runs, choose a variety of surfaces on which to run. All-road will be too unrelenting, but all-country may be an unduly tough test for tendons and ligaments unused to uneven ground for such a long period.

Warm-up:

Warm-down:

Other exercise today:

Run details:

Accompanied by:

Comments:

MONDAY

Thought for the Day:
Our greatest battles are those with our own minds
– Frank Jameson

STATISTICS

Date:

Time of day: AM/PM

Conditions:

Location:

Estimated distance: miles kilometres

Time (duration): hrs mins

Aims:

TRAINING TIP
Massage is an effective way of assisting muscle repair. Even self-administered massage can achieve this, if you take the time to learn. Browse the books available (the internet is no good for this – you need quality, portable reference material) and buy one.

Warm-up:

Warm-down:

Other exercise today:

Run details:

Accompanied by:

Comments:

TUESDAY

Thought for the Day:
That which is measured, improves
– Anon

STATISTICS

Date:

Time of day: AM/PM

Conditions:

Location:

Estimated distance: miles kilometres

Time (duration): hrs mins

Aims:

TRAINING TIP
Water in your shoes can cause blisters. There are such things as waterproof socks, which may prevent this (and provde greater comfort). The prices vary considerably, as does the quality of the product.

Warm-up:

Warm-down:

Other exercise today:

Run details:

Accompanied by:

Comments:

WEEK 5

WEDNESDAY

Thought for the Day:
The first wealth is health
– Ralph Waldo Emerson

STATISTICS

Date:

Time of day: AM/PM

Conditions:

Location:

Estimated distance: miles   kilometres

Time (duration):   hrs   mins

Aims:

TRAINING TIP
Check that the roads you regularly run on do not mean that you are always on the same camber (to the left if you run with traffic, to the right if you run facing). It is the surest path to injury.

Warm-up:

Warm-down:

Other exercise today:

Run details:

Accompanied by:

Comments:

THURSDAY

Thought for the Day:
Jog on, jog on, the footpath way,
Your sad tires in a mile-a.
– Shakespeare, *The Winter's Tale*

STATISTICS

Date:

Time of day: AM/PM

Conditions:

Location:

Estimated distance: miles   kilometres

Time (duration):   hrs   mins

Aims:

TRAINING TIP
When you lace your shoes, especially before a race, you may pull them so tight that they soon cause discomfort, and even injury to the tendons on top of your feet. Use a small sheet of foam to add extra cushioning.

Warm-up:

Warm-down:

Other exercise today:

Run details:

Accompanied by:

Comments:

WEEK 5

FRIDAY

Thought for the Day:
We do not stop playing because we grow old; we grow old because
we stop playing
– Anon

STATISTICS

Date:

Time of day: AM/PM

Conditions:

Location:

Estimated distance: miles kilometres

Time (duration): hrs mins

Aims:

TRAINING TIP

If you are now training regularly for the first time, consider getting a medical check just to ensure that some previously undetected condition is not emerging under your new exercise regime. Such a check may also give an indication of general health improvement.

Warm-up:

Warm-down:

Other exercise today:

Run details:

Accompanied by:

Comments:

SATURDAY

Thought for the Day:
People are always blaming their circumstances. They look for circumstances they want, and if they can't find them, make them
– George Bernard Shaw

STATISTICS

Date:

Time of day: AM/PM

Conditions:

Location:

Estimated distance: miles kilometres

Time (duration): hrs mins

Aims:

TRAINING TIP

Effective relaxation may be more difficult than it appears. If you encounter difficulties, explore possibilities of learing this skill through yoga classes or following the Alexander technique, etc. What works for you is worth doing.

Warm-up:

Warm-down:

Other exercise today:

Run details:

Accompanied by:

Comments:

WEEK 5

WEEK 6

11 weeks to go

To help you cope with a longer run you can increase the duration and lessen the intensity of your effort. In other words, it may turn into a long walk with some running, rather than a long run with some walking. You should now be able to cope with 90 minutes of running, and to extend the session to three hours you will have to walk for more of the time than has previously been necessary. You should aim for an average pace of at least 5 miles per hour. Anything much less than this could be achieved by walking only.

Any greater distance provides a bonus to set yourself up for future long runs. It will make it easier to convert 'time on your feet' to time spent running.

The midweek run should be lengthened. If it is more convenient, switch days so that you run longer on the Thursday. The increased length of the run is a minor test in itself, but there is another purpose to be served by varying the pace of this run. You will start to use it to introduce more variation into your training. To do this with least effort (although increased effort is the point of the exercise) at first just use a more hilly route.

Suggested Routine

SUNDAY	Longer run – 90 minutes, or 3 hours' walk, running some sections (target distance: 15 miles)
MONDAY	recovery
TUESDAY	30 minutes running
WEDNESDAY	45 minutes running, varying effort: on hills
THURSDAY	30 minutes running
FRIDAY	recovery
SATURDAY	recovery

WEEK 6

SUNDAY

Thought for the Day:
Every battle is won before it is fought
– Sun Tzu, *The Art of War*

STATISTICS

Date:
Time of day: AM/PM
Conditions:

Location:
Estimated distance: miles kilometres
Time (duration): hrs mins

Aims:

TRAINING TIP

Long runs may take you far from home. If you then run into trouble – injury, a dog bite or anything unforeseen – you may need to get back by other means. Take some money – at least the price of a phone call – for use in such circumstances.

Warm-up:
Warm-down:
Other exercise today:

Run details:

Accompanied by:

Comments:

MONDAY

Thought for the Day:
There is only one real failure in life and that is not to be true to the best we know
– Frederick Farrar

STATISTICS

Date:

Time of day: AM/PM

Conditions:

Location:

Estimated distance: miles   kilometres

Time (duration): hrs   mins

Aims:

TRAINING TIP

Paula Radcliffe's famous ice baths may be too much, but you can reduce micro muscle damage by submerging your lower legs in cold water after racing or hard training. Even better if you can do this while the upper body is horizontal.

Warm-up:

Warm-down:

Other exercise today:

Run details:

Accompanied by:

Comments:

TUESDAY

Thought for the Day:
No person who is occupied doing a very difficult thing, and doing it well, loses his self-respect
– George Bernard Shaw

STATISTICS

Date:

Time of day: AM/PM

Conditions:

Location:

Estimated distance: miles   kilometres

Time (duration): hrs   mins

Aims:

TRAINING TIP

Always look on the bright side of life: if it is raining it will keep you cool; if it is hot, your muscles will be loose.

Warm-up:

Warm-down:

Other exercise today:

Run details:

Accompanied by:

Comments:

WEEK 6

WEDNESDAY	**THURSDAY**

Thought for the Day:
To improve is to change. To be perfect is to change often
– Winston Churchill

Thought for the Day:
"O Oysters," said the Carpenter, "you've had a pleasant run! Shall we be trotting home again?" But the answer, there was none
– Lewis Carroll, *Through the Looking Glass*

STATISTICS

STATISTICS

Date:

Time of day: AM/PM

Conditions:

Location:

Estimated distance: miles   kilometres

Time (duration):   hrs   mins

Aims:

Date:

Time of day: AM/PM

Conditions:

Location:

Estimated distance: miles   kilometres

Time (duration):   hrs   mins

Aims:

TRAINING TIP

The first thing you want to do after a run may be to eat, but first allow yourself to work off the sweat. That way the blood can get to the right place at the right time to digest your food.

TRAINING TIP

Much of the mental effort of running comes before you get out of the front door. Realise this, and act upon it, and you'll be out running in quick time.

Warm-up:

Warm-down:

Other exercise today:

Run details:

Accompanied by:

Comments:

Warm-up:

Warm-down:

Other exercise today:

Run details:

Accompanied by:

Comments:

WEEK 6

FRIDAY

Thought for the Day:
Nothing great was ever achieved without enthusiasm
– Ralph Waldo Emerson

STATISTICS

Date:

Time of day: AM/PM

Conditions:

Location:

Estimated distance: miles kilometres

Time (duration): hrs mins

Aims:

TRAINING TIP

When you read a running tip, be aware it is for general application. Many may not be best applied to your own situation. Always use your own intelligence to apply helpfully meant advice.

Warm-up:

Warm-down:

Other exercise today:

Run details:

Accompanied by:

Comments:

SATURDAY

Thought for the Day:
This is not the end. it is not even the beginning of the end. But it is, perhaps, the end of the beginning
– Winston Churchill

STATISTICS

Date:

Time of day: AM/PM

Conditions:

Location:

Estimated distance: miles kilometres

Time (duration): hrs mins

Aims:

TRAINING TIP

Keep spare safety pins pinned to your running vest or shorts. When you run a race it will save you the trouble of hunting around for them before the start.

Warm-up:

Warm-down:

Other exercise today:

Run details:

Accompanied by:

Comments:

WEEK 6

WEEK 7

10 weeks to go

The long outing of the previous weekend should have given you some confidence with which to tackle a continuous run for a lesser time – even though this is two hours. If you find you have to walk at times, then try to keep these sections to a minimum.

Another way of encouraging yourself into running non-stop is to do another race – this time a half marathon. You may not be able to complete it in the target two hours, and you should not strain to do so. The aim is to run for two hours or, if necessary, more. The need to complete the particular distance arises from using the race as a means to help you fulfil the training programme. It is not the prime objective of the training programme. If you suffer stiffness afterwards, re-arrange your training week to allow for two days recovery.

Continue to vary the midweek session. Use a similar hilly route as last week, but this time consciously increase your effort as you climb the hills. Ease off after you reach the top. This is the opposite of what you should do in long runs, where you need to reduce effort on the hills.

Suggested Routine

SUNDAY	Longer run – 2 hours, trying to avoid walking or do this session as a half marathon race – remember to do a short warm up and warm down before & after
MONDAY	recovery
TUESDAY	30 minutes running (or recovery if still stiff)
WEDNESDAY	50 minutes running – varying effort (or switch sessions with Thursday)
THURSDAY	30 minutes running
FRIDAY	recovery
SATURDAY	30 minutes running

SUNDAY

Thought for the Day:
Success seems to be largely a matter of hanging on after others have let go
– William Feather

STATISTICS

Date:

Time of day: AM/PM

Conditions:

Location:

Estimated distance: miles   kilometres

Time (duration): hrs   mins

Aims:

TRAINING TIP
Running behind someone requires less effort than running in front of them. If you want to be 'carried' through a run, tuck in behind a group and just keep pace. It is physiacally and mentally less taxing than leading.

Warm-up:

Warm-down:

Other exercise today:

Run details:

Accompanied by:

Comments:

W E E K 7

MONDAY

Thought for the Day:
He that fights and runs away may live to fight another day
– Anon

STATISTICS

Date:

Time of day: AM/PM

Conditions:

Location:

Estimated distance: miles kilometres

Time (duration): hrs mins

Aims:

TRAINING TIP

If you are suffering from particular soreness after running – a knee or heel, perhaps – then apply ice immediately after you finish the run. It is the most effective way of reducing swelling and inflammation.

Warm-up:

Warm-down:

Other exercise today:

Run details:

Accompanied by:

Comments:

TUESDAY

Thought for the Day:
Failure is the opportunity to begin again more efficiently
– Henry Ford

STATISTICS

Date:

Time of day: AM/PM

Conditions:

Location:

Estimated distance: miles kilometres

Time (duration): hrs mins

Aims:

TRAINING TIPS

When you finish a run, with your muscles suffering from trauma, you need to divert the blood from engulfing the damaged area and causing swelling. The simplest way is to lie on your back on the floor with your feet propped up against a wall.

Warm-up:

Warm-down:

Other exercise today:

Run details:

Accompanied by:

Comments:

WEEK 7

WEDNESDAY	**THURSDAY**

Thought for the Day:
"Will you walk a little faster?" said a whiting to a snail
– Lewis Carroll, *Alice's Adventures in Wonderland*

Thought for the Day:
Training is everything
– Mark Twain

STATISTICS

Date:

Time of day: AM/PM

Conditions:

Location:

Estimated distance: miles   kilometres

Time (duration):   hrs   mins

Aims:

STATISTICS

Date:

Time of day: AM/PM

Conditions:

Location:

Estimated distance: miles   kilometres

Time (duration):   hrs   mins

Aims:

TRAINING TIP

Practise changing pace to give yourself a tactical range. When over-taking someone in a race you may need to rest a while just slightly behind them, and then sweep past at an increased pace, giving them little chance to respond until you have a clear lead.

TRAINING TIP

For normal running, try to maximise the amount you do on grass. This is a softer, kinder surface, and is more variable. This forces yoour small balancing and supporting muscles to do some of the work, and keeps them in condition.

Warm-up:

Warm-down:

Other exercise today:

Run details:

Accompanied by:

Comments:

Warm-up:

Warm-down:

Other exercise today:

Run details:

Accompanied by:

Comments:

WEEK 7

FRIDAY

Thought for the Day:
**How many roads must a man walk down,
Before you call him a man?**
– Bob Dylan, 'Blowing in the Wind'

STATISTICS

Date:

Time of day: AM/PM

Conditions:

Location:

Estimated distance: miles   kilometres

Time (duration): hrs   mins

Aims:

TRAINING TIP
Variety is the spice of life. Map out new roads to run down, new parks to pass through. You may at first take longer to cover the distance, but you then have a new marker for subsequent improvement.

Warm-up:

Warm-down:

Other exercise today:

Run details:

Accompanied by:

Comments:

SATURDAY

Thought for the Day:
**Oh! How I hate to get up in the morning,
Oh! How I'd love to remain in bed**
– Irving Berlin

STATISTICS

Date:

Time of day: AM/PM

Conditions:

Location:

Estimated distance: miles   kilometres

Time (duration): hrs   mins

Aims:

TRAINING TIP
When you encounter other runners in training, catch up with them – take short cuts if necessary – or let them catch up with you. Engage them in conversation: "How far are you going?" However far it is, it will seem less in company.

Warm-up:

Warm-down:

Other exercise today:

Run details:

Accompanied by:

Comments:

WEEK 7

WEEK 8

9 weeks to go

In your long run you should concentrate on running for 2 hours, without walking. Use what strategies you can to avoid taking breaks, but it may still be worth walking up any steep gradients.

You should continue to develop your midweek run. Anticipate when you will increase your effort each time and for how long. You may even find it helpful to time each effort. Don't restrict yourself to attacking the uphill sections. You can also increase your pace on the flat for a minute or two. To improve your leg speed you can incorporate faster efforts on gentle downhill stretches. By doing this you can run much faster without becoming out of breath. Try to do this on grass or other soft surfaces, as the increased force with which your feet hit the ground could lead to injury on hard pavements.

The variation of the midweek run serves several purposes. You work on your speed with the gently downhill efforts, you develop your strength by attacking the hills, and you build your endurance through the overall effect of the session. The constant surging you introduce into your run is a recognised technique first developed in Scandinavia and called "fartlek", or "speed play".

Suggested Routine

SUNDAY	Longer run – 2 hours
MONDAY	recovery
TUESDAY	30 minutes running
WEDNESDAY	50 minutes "fartlek"
THURSDAY	30 minutes running
FRIDAY	recovery
SATURDAY	30 minutes running

WEEK 8

SUNDAY

Thought for the Day:
Keep right on to the end of the road,
Keep right on to the end
– Sir Harry Lauder (song)

STATISTICS

Date:

Time of day: AM/PM

Conditions:

Location:

Estimated distance: miles   kilometres

Time (duration):   hrs   mins

Aims:

TRAINING TIP

On runs, and especially on long runs, carry some form of identification with you. You never know when this may be of service. A convenient form, purpose-designed for runners, is the Cramtag. Check www.jpanton.freeserve.co.uk/cramtag.html

Warm-up:

Warm-down:

Other exercise today:

Run details:

Accompanied by:

Comments:

MONDAY

Thought for the Day:
He who has never hoped can never despair
– George Bernard Shaw

STATISTICS

Date:

Time of day: AM/PM

Conditions:

Location:

Estimated distance: miles kilometres

Time (duration): hrs mins

Aims:

TRAINING TIP

Recovery doesn't mean slumping in a chair all day; it can be active. As running gets you used to expending more energy, you will most likely find yourself impatient with the sluggard's habits of waiting for a lift to go up two floors or standing still on the escalator.

Warm-up:

Warm-down:

Other exercise today:

Run details:

Accompanied by:

Comments:

TUESDAY

Thought for the Day:
Labor omnia vicit ("Toil overcomes all")
– Virgil

STATISTICS

Date:

Time of day: AM/PM

Conditions:

Location:

Estimated distance: miles kilometres

Time (duration): hrs mins

Aims:

TRAINING TIP

If those laces are still unravelling then buy some lace locks, another gadget pioneered by time-conscious triathletes that cost next to nothing.

Warm-up:

Warm-down:

Other exercise today:

Run details:

Accompanied by:

Comments:

WEEK 8

WEDNESDAY

Thought for the Day:
You see, it takes all the running you can do to stay in the same place.
If you want to get somewhere else, you must run at least twice as fast
– Lewis Carroll

STATISTICS

Date:

Time of day: AM/PM

Conditions:

Location:

Estimated distance: miles kilometres

Time (duration): hrs mins

Aims:

TRAINING TIP
If you are temporarily unable to train but are desperate to maintain condition during your layoff, it may be worth using a health club to do repetitions on an exercise bike, or using a wet vest in the pool. There are also some machines that allow you to run with no impact.

Warm-up:

Warm-down:

Other exercise today:

Run details:

Accompanied by:

Comments:

THURSDAY

Thought for the Day:
The reward of a thing well done is to have done it
– Ralph Waldo Emerson

STATISTICS

Date:

Time of day: AM/PM

Conditions:

Location:

Estimated distance: miles kilometres

Time (duration): hrs mins

Aims:

TRAINING TIP
Buy a second pair of shoes and use them alternately with your normal pair. Use the lighter and less supportive pair for your shorter runs, and the more supportive pair for longer runs. Don't use either for anything other than running.

Warm-up:

Warm-down:

Other exercise today:

Run details:

Accompanied by:

Comments:

FRIDAY

Thought for the Day:
Procrastination is the thief of time
– Edward Young

STATISTICS

Date:

Time of day: AM/PM

Conditions:

Location:

Estimated distance: miles   kilometres

Time (duration):   hrs   mins

Aims:

TRAINING TIP

By all means clean and dry your shoes, but not in a dryer or on a radiator. Heat (and extreme cold) will make the midsole lose is shock-absorbing qualities.

Warm-up:

Warm-down:

Other exercise today:

Run details:

Accompanied by:

Comments:

SATURDAY

Thought for the Day:
Footfalls echo in the memory
Down the passage which we did not take
– T S Eliot

STATISTICS

Date:

Time of day: AM/PM

Conditions:

Location:

Estimated distance: miles   kilometres

Time (duration):   hrs   mins

Aims:

TRAINING TIP

Have you been using a heart rate monitor? You can more closely monitor your effort while running and learn more about yourself. You can also check your heart rate first thing in the morning, as an early warning of any bug you may have picked up.

Warm-up:

Warm-down:

Other exercise today:

Run details:

Accompanied by:

Comments:

WEEK 8

WEEK 9

SUNDAY

8 weeks to go

Now you have tried running without a break for two hours, it may again be worth varying your approach as you did a few weeks ago. By including walking, try to double the time of your session, but don't worry too much about your pace. If you run for a significant amount of the time, when you feel like doing so, you will boost your average pace above what you could manage even as a fast walk. On this basis, 5mph is a realistic target. If you can keep this going for four hours, then you will have covered 20 miles.

This is often as much as a runner will attempt to do at one time before a marathon. The conditions on race day can be relied upon to draw out a little bit more from you than you can volunteer in a training session. If you can manage 20miles in training, completing a marathon should not be too difficult for you.

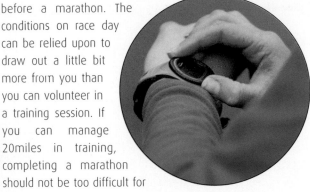

If you do not like walking during your runs, then try to extend the duration of your run, by another half hour. There is no point in running for the two hours to which you have become accustomed, and then walking for half an hour. Mix any necessary walking into the run a little at a time.

The rest of the week can be active recovery. Extend yourself a little on the fartlek session, but otherwise do just one easy run.

Suggested Routine

SUNDAY	4 hours walk, running sections: target distance 20 miles or 2.5 hours consistent run, walking only if necessary
MONDAY	recovery
TUESDAY	30 minutes running
WEDNESDAY	recovery
THURSDAY	50 minutes fartlek
FRIDAY	recovery
SATURDAY	recovery

Thought for the Day:
There is more to life than increasing its speed
– Mahatma Gandhi

STATISTICS

Date:

Time of day: AM/PM

Conditions:

Location:

Estimated distance: miles kilometres

Time (duration): hrs mins

Aims:

TRAINING TIP

When you are feeling pains, do they ease off with the distance covered, or do they get worse? The first sort are probably not storing up trouble for the future, but the second kind certainly will be doing so. With both make sure there is no deterioration later.

Warm-up:

Warm-down:

Other exercise today:

Run details:

Accompanied by:

Comments:

MONDAY

Thought for the Day:
Time goes, you say? Ah no!
Alas, time stays. We go
– Austin Dobson

STATISTICS

Date:

Time of day: AM/PM

Conditions:

Location:

Estimated distance: miles kilometres

Time (duration): hrs mins

Aims:

TRAINING TIP

If you have acquired an injury – a pain which persists – then don't just go and get the symptoms treated for temporary relief. To set your mind permanently at rest you need to trace the root cause. For example, many muscle problems may result from your running style.

Warm-up:

Warm-down:

Other exercise today:

Run details:

Accompanied by:

Comments:

TUESDAY

Thought for the Day:
Life is one long process of getting tired
– Samuel Butler

STATISTICS

Date:

Time of day: AM/PM

Conditions:

Location:

Estimated distance: miles kilometres

Time (duration): hrs mins

Aims:

TRAINING TIP

When running at night or at dusk, make sure you are seen. Wear light coloured gear. Make sure your shoes and trackters have some fluorescent edging so that you will be caught in car headlights very far ahead.

Warm-up:

Warm-down:

Other exercise today:

Run details:

Accompanied by:

Comments:

WEEK 9

WEDNESDAY

Thought for the Day:
The golden rule is that there are no golden rules
– George Bernard Shaw

STATISTICS

Date:

Time of day: AM/PM

Conditions:

Location:

Estimated distance: miles kilometres

Time (duration): hrs mins

Aims:

TRAINING TIP

If you are still increasing your training mileage, do not do so by more than ten per cent a week. If you wish to take advice from coach GBS (above), then stretch it to 15 percent – no more (that is an iron rule – not a golden one).

warm-up:

warm-down:

Other exercise today:

Run details:

Accompanied by:

Comments:

THURSDAY

Thought for the Day:
The credit belongs to those in the arena, who strive valiantly; who, if they fail, fail while daring greatly
– Theodore Roosevelt

STATISTICS

Date:

Time of day: AM/PM

Conditions:

Location:

Estimated distance: miles kilometres

Time (duration): hrs mins

Aims:

TRAINING TIP

Try to relax during your training – even the hard stuff. Self–analyse your style and see how you can reduce tension. Pay particular attention to your shoulder and neck muscles, which can often tense unneccesarily.

warm-up:

warm-down:

Other exercise today:

Run details:

Accompanied by:

Comments:

FRIDAY

Thought for the Day:
Success is relative
– T S Eliot

STATISTICS

Date:

Time of day: AM/PM

Conditions:

Location:

Estimated distance: miles   kilometres

Time (duration):   hrs   mins

Aims:

TRAINING TIP
If you think you may be getting a cold (that tell–tale dryness in the nasal passages), stuff yourself with Vitamin C. Take 200mg tablets morning, noon and night, if not more frequently. This may block symptoms, or at least render them less severe.

warm-up:

warm-down:

Other exercise today:

Run details:

Accompanied by:

Comments:

SATURDAY

Thought for the Day:
Man's main task in life is to give birth to himself;
to become what he potentially is
– Erich Fromm

STATISTICS

Date:

Time of day: AM/PM

Conditions:

Location:

Estimated distance: miles   kilometres

Time (duration):   hrs   mins

Aims:

TRAINING TIP
Time to check your shoes again. Stand vertically and get someone to see if your feet rest evenly in the shoes. Any irregularity could mean that the midsole has deformed through use. If in doubt, go back to the good folks at your local runner–run running shop.

warm-up:

warm-down:

Other exercise today:

Run details:

Accompanied by:

Comments:

WEEK 9

WEEK 10

SUNDAY

Thought for the Day:
Sunday clears away the rust of the whole week
– Joseph Addison

STATISTICS

Date:

Time of day: AM/PM

Conditions:

Location:

Estimated distance: miles   kilometres

Time (duration):   hrs   mins

Aims:

TRAINING TIP

When you run – particularly when you run long – warn people. Let them know where you are going. Then they will know where they should send the search party, should you not return on schedule.

warm-up:

warm-down:

Other exercise today:

Run details:

Accompanied by:

Comments:

7 weeks to go

This week is a replica of the previous week. Having rehearsed it once, you should be able to improve on it this time around. You should have taken enough rest during the previous week to feel fresh enough to renew the challenge of completing a 2.5 hour run.

Use your experience of the previous week to judge how you can best cope with the length of this session. When do you first start to feel tired, and slow down? Could fatigue be put off by taking a short walking break beforehand? When you have taken one break, at what intervals do you feel it necessary to take more of them? How long are they compared to the sections you run? Try to find answers to these questions and use them to come up with a planned approach to your long runs. Don't take haphazard walking breaks any longer, whenever the idea appeals. Discipline your breaks into a regular pattern and try to stick to it – although you should always be prepared to save yourself up steep hills.

You need to find a realistic rhythm to your expenditure of energy, so that you never become completely drained. Ideally this will be at running pace, but an efficient mix of running and walking will not slow you by very much in your marathon attempt.

Suggested Routine

SUNDAY	Longer run – 2.5 hours
MONDAY	recovery
TUESDAY	30 minutes running
WEDNESDAY	1 hour fartlek
THURSDAY	30 minutes running
FRIDAY	recovery
SATURDAY	recovery

WEEK 10

MONDAY

Thought for the Day:
I find the great thing in this world is not so much where we stand, as in what direction we are moving
– Oliver Wendell Holmes

STATISTICS

Date:

Time of day: AM/PM

Conditions:

Location:

Estimated distance: miles   kilometres

Time (duration): hrs   mins

Aims:

TRAINING TIP

Face oncoming traffic. Unless you have to negotiate tight bends, when you will get greater visibility by being on the opposite side, run against traffic. This gives you the means to sidestep homicidal drivers – and there are more than you think!

warm-up:

warm-down:

Other exercise today:

Run details:

Accompanied by:

Comments:

TUESDAY

Thought for the Day:
Courage is the thing. All goes if courage goes
– Sir J M Barrie

STATISTICS

Date:

Time of day: AM/PM

Conditions:

Location:

Estimated distance: miles   kilometres

Time (duration): hrs   mins

Aims:

TRAINING TIP

Icing sore body parts may combat inflammation, but to speed recovery of already healing injuries you need to increase the blood flow. In such cases apply hot and cold treatment after running. Alternate two minutes of a hot shower with two minutes of ice.

warm-up:

warm-down:

Other exercise today:

Run details:

Accompanied by:

Comments:

WEEK 10

WEDNESDAY

Thought for the Day:
The woods are lovely dark and deep, but I have promises to keep
And miles to go before I sleep
– Robert Frost

STATISTICS

Date:

Time of day: AM/PM

Conditions:

Location:

Estimated distance: miles kilometres

Time (duration): hrs mins

Aims:

TRAINING TIP
Should you find your performances deteriorating inexplicably, this could be anaemia. Take one tablet of Ferrograd C daily for five days, then every other day for 10 days. If this doesn't solve it, you may have another ailment – but this treatment does no harm.

warm-up:

warm-down:

Other exercise today:

Run details:

Accompanied by:

Comments:

THURSDAY

Thought for the Day:
Mud! Mud! Glorious mud!
Nothing quite like it for cooling the blood
– Michael Flanders and Donald Swan

STATISTICS

Date:

Time of day: AM/PM

Conditions:

Location:

Estimated distance: miles kilometres

Time (duration): hrs mins

Aims:

TRAINING TIP
When you run downhill, adjust your style. If it is steep you need to save yourself from braking. Flailing arms are no disgrace – a temporary but flagrantly inefficient style may avoid some of the conscious effort of slowing yourself down.

warm-up:

warm-down:

Other exercise today:

Run details:

Accompanied by:

Comments:

WEEK 10

FRIDAY

Thought for the Day:
Live all you can; it is a mistake not to
– Henry Miller

STATISTICS

Date:

Time of day: AM/PM

Conditions:

Location:

Estimated distance: miles   kilometres

Time (duration): hrs   mins

Aims:

TRAINING TIP
On your off–days, you may have exercised in other ways. "Cross training" is nothing more than making this a formal arrangement: on days when you don't run, you do another recorded bout of car-dio–vascular exercise – swimming, rowing, cycling, etc.

warm-up:

warm-down:

Other exercise today:

Run details:

Accompanied by:

Comments:

SATURDAY

Thought for the Day:
Far away is close at hand
– Robert Graves

STATISTICS

Date:

Time of day: AM/PM

Conditions:

Location:

Estimated distance: miles   kilometres

Time (duration): hrs   mins

Aims:

TRAINING TIP
The heel counters of your shoes are made of rigid plastic (all brands) and may rub. if this happens, the inner cushioning will wear thin, and your heel may be suffering injury without you noticing. The solution is to drastically cut down the rigid plastic with a scalpel.

warm-up:

warm-down:

Other exercise today:

Run details:

Accompanied by:

Comments:

WEEK 10

WEEK 11

SUNDAY

6 weeks to go

What follows looks like a recovery week programme, but it isn't. You only have three sessions, but two of these are demanding efforts. This week's long run is the first of two at maximum length of three hours. The second one, three weeks later, should be easier to complete. If you have kept extending your long run as suggested you should not have undue physical

difficulty in running for three hours. But your mind may tell you differently.

Much of the difficulty in completing a marathon lies in your head. Once you are inwardly convinced that you can do it, everything else follows. It does not fall into place automatically, but it provides a secure base for your preparation. Once you have completed this three–hour run, you should have little doubt that you are capable of running a marathon.

But first you must tackle this run. One way to focus your mind on the task of completing any long run is to plan a route from a distant point back to your house. You have an obvious target to aim for. You could take a train 20 miles up the line and follow a parallel, fairly direct, route home on footpaths and quiet roads. If you really need to quit, you will be able to catch a train from one of the intermediate stations, as a last resort.

Take two days recovery and ease back to running by midweek, but maintain the controlled effort of your fartlek session to a lesser intensity.

Suggested Routine

SUNDAY	3 hours run
MONDAY	recovery
TUESDAY	recovery
WEDNESDAY	30 minutes running
THURSDAY	1 hour running, varying pace
FRIDAY	recovery
SATURDAY	recovery

Thought for the Day:
The journey of a thousand miles begins with a single step
– Lao Tzu

STATISTICS

Date:

Time of day: AM/PM

Conditions:

Location:

Estimated distance: miles   kilometres

Time (duration):   hrs   mins

Aims:

TRAINING TIP
After your long run, put your feet up for 10–15 minutes, then take a high carbohydrate snack, with plenty of water. If you then have a long, leisurely warm bath you will quite likely doze off easily afterwards. By the time you wake up you should feel substantially recovered.

warm-up:

warm-down:

Other exercise today:

Run details:

Accompanied by:

Comments:

MONDAY

Thought for the Day:
Philosophy is the replacement of category–habits by category–disciplines
– Gilbert Ryle

STATISTICS

Date:

Time of day:　　　　　AM/PM

Conditions:

Location:

Estimated distance:　　　miles　　　kilometres

Time (duration):　　　hrs　　　mins

Aims:

TRAINING TIP

If you suffer from asthma, and get occasional severe attacks where temporarily you cannot breathe, check out the Bowen technique. This employs a specific manipulation to release the spasm.

warm-up:

warm-down:

Other exercise today:

Run details:

Accompanied by:

Comments:

TUESDAY

Thought for the Day:
Experience is never limited, and it is never complete
– Henry James

STATISTICS

Date:

Time of day:　　　　　AM/PM

Conditions:

Location:

Estimated distance:　　　miles　　　kilometres

Time (duration):　　　hrs　　　mins

Aims:

TRAINING TIP

Even out your energy intake. Avoid heavy evening meals you can't digest before sleeping. Eat during the day when you are hungry. Snack on dried or raw fruit, and discover the joys of afternoon tea.

warm-up:

warm-down:

Other exercise today:

Run details:

Accompanied by:

Comments:

WEEK 11

WEDNESDAY	**THURSDAY**

Thought for the Day:
Lead me from death to life, from falsehood to truth.
Lead me from despair to hope, from fear to trust
– Satish Kumar

Thought for the Day:
So many paths that wind and wind
– Ella Wheeler Wilcox

STATISTICS

STATISTICS

Date:

Time of day: AM/PM

Conditions:

Location:

Estimated distance: miles   kilometres

Time (duration): hrs   mins

Aims:

Date:

Time of day: AM/PM

Conditions:

Location:

Estimated distance: miles   kilometres

Time (duration): hrs   mins

Aims:

TRAINING TIP

If you have to run on busy streets minimise your exposure to pollutants by staying well away from the kerb, closer to the buildings. Try to run early – and on hot, still days consider putting your run off altogether.

TRAINING TIP

Become an all-weather runner. If it is raining, there's more oxygen in the air for you. If it's windy, that gives you a chance for resistance training. If it's hot, you can tune up your body's cooling system. You only need forfeit a run when there's a lightning storm.

warm-up:

warm-down:

Other exercise today:

Run details:

Accompanied by:

Comments:

warm-up:

warm-down:

Other exercise today:

Run details:

Accompanied by:

Comments:

WEEK 11

FRIDAY

Thought for the Day:
No one can make you feel inferior without your consent
– Eleanor Roosevelt

STATISTICS

Date: ....

Time of day: .... AM/PM ....

Conditions: ....
....

Location: ....

Estimated distance: .... miles .... kilometres

Time (duration): .... hrs .... mins

Aims: ....
....
....
....

TRAINING TIP

You don't have to restrict stretching to pre–and post–run. Particularly if you are suffering from tight muscles, use any spare time you may have. While watching TV, while waiting for a bus or train, or while waiting for anything.

warm-up: ....

warm-down: ....

Other exercise today: ....
....

Run details: ....
....
....
....
....
....

Accompanied by: ....

Comments: ....
....
....
....
....
....

SATURDAY

Thought for the Day:
I wake to sleep, and take my waking slow. I feel my fate in what I cannot fear. I learn by going where I have to go.
–Theodore Roethke, *The Waking*

STATISTICS

Date: ....

Time of day: .... AM/PM ....

Conditions: ....
....

Location: ....

Estimated distance: .... miles .... kilometres

Time (duration): .... hrs .... mins

Aims: ....
....
....
....

TRAINING TIP

Don't worry about sleeping. If your body really needs it, it will take it. If you can't sleep, just lie still and avoid complicated thoughts that are better addressed in daytime. If you cannot banish such thoughts, get up and read for a while.

warm-up: ....

warm-down: ....

Other exercise today: ....
....

Run details: ....
....
....
....
....
....

Accompanied by: ....

Comments: ....
....
....
....
....
....

WEEK 11

WEEK 12

SUNDAY

5 weeks to go

Last week was a big physical effort, and probably mentally taxing, too. Races also demand effort and concentration, but in a very different way to long runs. With last week's run behind you, you should be confident that you can complete a half marathon, and probably run it a lot more effectively than you could in any earlier attempt.

A half marathon race is the closest you will come to your marathon experience until the appointed day. It is only half the

distance, but the other conditions are very similar. Pick a race which is similar in character to the marathon you will run. Remember to tell yourself throughout that this is only half what you will do in five weeks' time, and control your level of effort accordingly.

Jog a mile as a warm-up, but start slowly. Don't fight your way past people if it is crowded. Take drinks at the refreshment stations along the route. Try to finish with something to spare (don't worry now whether the 'something' would be enough to take you another 13 miles). Force yourself to jog slowly for 10–15 minutes afterwards as a warm down.

Assist your recovery the following day by taking some alternative exercise. Swimming is ideal, cycling also good. Treating yourself to a massage will also help (you may be able to get this after the race, but it will be a short session). Continue recovery through the week by running only gently.

Suggested Routine

SUNDAY	Race? Half marathon. warm up for a mile, and try to jog afterwards as a "warm down"
MONDAY	recovery – try swimming or cycling
TUESDAY	recovery
WEDNESDAY	30 minutes running, omit if muscles are still stiff
THURSDAY	1 hour running
FRIDAY	recovery
SATURDAY	30 minutes running

WEEK 12

Thought for the Day:
Achivement is largely the product of steadily raising one's levels of aspiration
– Jack Nicklaus

STATISTICS

Date:

Time of day: AM/PM

Conditions:

Location:

Estimated distance: miles   kilometres

Time (duration):   hrs   mins

Aims:

TRAINING TIP
Watch your step: you only need to turn your ankle to put yourself out of the big event. Fix your eyes three metres ahead of you and watch carefully for broken pavements, tree roots, etc.

warm-up:

warm-down:

Other exercise today:

Run details:

Accompanied by:

Comments:

MONDAY

Thought for the Day:
Climb ev'ry mountain, ford ev'ry stream
Follow ev'ry rainbow, 'till you find your dream
– Oscar Hammerstein II

STATISTICS

Date:

Time of day: AM/PM

Conditions:

Location:

Estimated distance: miles kilometres

Time (duration): hrs mins

Aims:

TRAINING TIP

Sense an oncoming cold? Eat a spicy curry to clear the passages. Take some hot, steamy drinks for a parallel effect. And pack in your vitamin C. The rest is fate.

warm-up:

warm-down:

Other exercise today:

Run details:

Accompanied by:

Comments:

TUESDAY

Thought for the Day:
The poetry of motion
– Kenneth Grahame

STATISTICS

Date:

Time of day: AM/PM

Conditions:

Location:

Estimated distance: miles kilometres

Time (duration): hrs mins

Aims:

TRAINING TIP

Make sure you read through all the instructions you have received from the marathon organisers. You would be surprised at how few people do so, yet you can save yourself much last-minute anxiety through knowing what to expect, and what to do.

warm-up:

warm-down:

Other exercise today:

Run details:

Accompanied by:

Comments:

WEEK 12

WEDNESDAY

Thought for the Day:
It is only a step from the sublime to the ridiculous
– Napoleon Bonaparte

STATISTICS

Date:

Time of day: AM/PM

Conditions:

Location:

Estimated distance: miles kilometres

Time (duration): hrs mins

Aims:

TRAINING TIP

Staying healthy for the next month is becoming very important. Reduce the chances of catching an infection by getting plenty of sleep, avoiding crowded situations and washing your hands regularly.

warm-up:

warm-down:

Other exercise today:

Run details:

Accompanied by:

Comments:

THURSDAY

Thought for the Day:
It is good to be out on the road, and going one knows not where
– John Masefield

STATISTICS

Date:

Time of day: AM/PM

Conditions:

Location:

Estimated distance: miles kilometres

Time (duration): hrs mins

Aims:

TRAINING TIP

If your form has taken a nosedive, you could be overdoing things. Recover condition by taking a complete break for a few days. You will be losing little in training, and maybe gaining the renewed impetus you need.

warm-up:

warm-down:

Other exercise today:

Run details:

Accompanied by:

Comments:

WEEK 12

FRIDAY

Thought for the Day:
What was hard to bear is sweet to remember
– Portuguese proverb

STATISTICS

Date:

Time of day: AM/PM

Conditions:

Location:

Estimated distance: miles kilometres

Time (duration): hrs mins

Aims:

TRAINING TIP

Now you are only a month away from the marathon, revisit your earlier ambitions. If you can estimate a likely time to aim for, this will focus your effort more forcefully than the simple desire to last the course that you may have started off with.

warm-up:

warm-down:

Other exercise today:

Run details:

Accompanied by:

Comments:

SATURDAY

Thought for the Day:
I travel light; as light, that is, as a man can travel who will
Still carry his body around because of its sentimental value
– Christopher Fry

STATISTICS

Date:

Time of day: AM/PM

Conditions:

Location:

Estimated distance: miles kilometres

Time (duration): hrs mins

Aims:

TRAINING TIP

When the clocks change, you have a choice: if they go forward (and you lose an hour) then adapt to the new time right away. If they go back, and you gain an hour, then get up that hour earlier and make use of the time with which you have been presented.

warm-up:

warm-down:

Other exercise today:

Run details:

Accompanied by:

Comments:

WEEK 12

WEEK 13

4 weeks to go

You should have been running easily enough during the previous week to feel recovered from the hard training you have been doing over the last few weeks. This week starts the final push towards the marathon, with most of the work being done in the next two weeks.

Go back to a long run of "only" 2.5 hours, or repeat the 4–hour run/walk. Either of these sessions will deliver benefits to you, but you should be able to handle them without strain. If you run, tell yourself that you have previously run further. If you run/walk, remind yourself that you have run continuously for almost as long, and should not need too many walking breaks.

You should only need one day to recover, and by Wednesday you should be ready for your regular fartlek run. By now you may have found that even within the loose "speed–play" format of this session, you have started to run to a fixed pattern, especially if you are running circuits in a park. There is no problem with this, and it is a development towards a genuine "repetition" session geared towards developing speed endurance. Such a session may consist of repeatedly running fast for (say) four min-utes, with a two-minute recovery between these efforts (generally, recover for half of the time of the effort).

Run easily the next day, and take a two-day rest – you will have earned it.

Suggested Routine

SUNDAY	Longer run, 2.5 hours or 4 hours run/walk
MONDAY	recovery
TUESDAY	30 minutes running
WEDNESDAY	1 hour fartlek
THURSDAY	30 minutes running
FRIDAY	recovery
SATURDAY	recovery

WEEK 13

SUNDAY

Thought for the Day:
**For men may come and men may go
But I go on forever
– Alfred Lord Tennyson**

STATISTICS

Date:

Time of day: AM/PM

Conditions:

Location:

Estimated distance: miles kilometres

Time (duration): hrs mins

Aims:

TRAINING TIP

If the sun is strong, you may consider using sunblock. This may be worthwhile for vulnerable parts like the nose and tips of ears, but any more general smearing may inhibit sweating. Avoid sunblock on the forehead: it channels sweat into your eyes.

warm-up:

warm-down:

Other exercise today:

Run details:

Accompanied by:

Comments:

MONDAY

Thought for the Day:
If you can't excel with talent, triumph with effort
– Weinbaum

STATISTICS

Date:

Time of day: AM/PM

Conditions:

Location:

Estimated distance: miles   kilometres

Time (duration): hrs   mins

Aims:

TRAINING TIP

Rein back on non–essential exercise. Walk up stairs, but don'r go up them two at a time. DON'T run for the bus or make too sudden moves, which can all–too easily end up in strains or full–blown injury.

warm-up:

warm-down:

Other exercise today:

Run details:

Accompanied by:

Comments:

TUESDAY

Thought for the Day:
Success is the sum of small efforts, repeated day in and day out
– Robert J Collier

STATISTICS

Date:

Time of day: AM/PM

Conditions:

Location:

Estimated distance: miles   kilometres

Time (duration): hrs   mins

Aims:

TRAINING TIP

Don't go for the shortest and tightest curve around the kerb of a turn. Go wide, swing into the kerb and then wide again, reducing the need to slow down. For a U–turn this does not apply: take the shortest route on the inside, as you will have to slow up anyway.

warm-up:

warm-down:

Other exercise today:

Run details:

Accompanied by:

Comments:

WEEK 13

WEDNESDAY

Thought for the Day:
Even if you are on the right track, you'll get
run over if you just sit there
– Arthur Godfrey

STATISTICS

Date:
Time of day: AM/PM
Conditions:

Location:
Estimated distance: miles kilometres
Time (duration): hrs mins

Aims:

TRAINING TIP
Sunglasses aren't just protection from the sun and glare. They can also keep insects and airborne debris out of your eyes – those nasty wraparound ones are especially effective for this.

warm-up:
warm-down:
Other exercise today:

Run details:

Accompanied by:

Comments:

THURSDAY

Thought for the Day:
Practice makes the master
– German proverb

STATISTICS

Date:
Time of day: AM/PM
Conditions:

Location:
Estimated distance: miles kilometres
Time (duration): hrs mins

Aims:

TRAINING TIP
Without sunblock, how do you protect yourself? By covering up. Wear a thin T-shirt rather than a vest. Wear a hat with a train. Or find a genuine reason to wear a cap with the peak at the back – to protect your neck from sunstroke.

warm-up:
warm-down:
Other exercise today:

Run details:

Accompanied by:

Comments:

WEEK 13

FRIDAY

Thought for the Day:
Action springs not from thought, but from a readiness for responsibility
– Dietrich Bonhoeffer

STATISTICS

Date:

Time of day: AM/PM

Conditions:

Location:

Estimated distance: miles   kilometres

Time (duration):   hrs   mins

Aims:

TRAINING TIP
As you rest more, sleep becomes even more important. Keep to a waking/sleeping routine that will see you through to race day. Make sure your bedroom is well-ventilated.

warm-up:

warm-down:

Other exercise today:

Run details:

Accompanied by:

Comments:

SATURDAY

Thought for the Day:
What would life be if we had no courage to attempt anything?
– Vincent van Gogh

STATISTICS

Date:

Time of day: AM/PM

Conditions:

Location:

Estimated distance: miles   kilometres

Time (duration):   hrs   mins

Aims:

TRAINING TIP
Don't plan on departing from your established routine at this late stage – it's much too late. Just do as you have done, and trust to fate.

warm-up:

warm-down:

Other exercise today:

Run details:

Accompanied by:

Comments:

WEEK 13

WEEK 14

SUNDAY

Thought for the Day:
Gwine to run all night, gwine to run all day
– S C Forster, 'Camptown Races'

STATISTICS

Date:

Time of day: AM/PM

Conditions:

Location:

Estimated distance: miles   kilometres

Time (duration): hrs   mins

Aims:

3 weeks to go

Start this week with your last really significant effort before the race itself. This is your second maximum–length run. It really should be a continuous run to best prepare you for the marathon itself. You may want to repeat your previous 3–hour route if this was a successful session before. If you do not feel that you have had enough practice in drinking while on the run, try to identify drinking fountains along the route. Most parks will have them, but they may not be in working order.

Take some other form of exercise the following day, like you did after running the half marathon. Non weight–bearing exercise like swimming or cycling is best. It will help your circulatory system without generating further temporary damage to the muscles. You may wish to do this for two days, but as you approach the marathon itself you will need to build in more rest to the schedule, and this means you do not need to replace running with other activities.

Do an easy run during the week and then complete your last fartlek session.

TRAINING TIP

It is reassuring to run a marathon when you know the lie of the land. If you do not live too far away, start your long run somewhere along the course, and run towards the finish. For convenience, you may need to enlist a driver's help.

warm-up:

warm-down:

Other exercise today:

Run details:

Accompanied by:

Comments:

Suggested Routine

SUNDAY	Long run – 3 hours
MONDAY	recovery – other activity
TUESDAY	recovery
WEDNESDAY	30 minutes running
THURSDAY	1 hour fartlek
FRIDAY	recovery
SATURDAY	30 minutes running

WEEK 14

MONDAY

Thought for the Day:
Life is a challenge – meet it.
Mother Teresa

STATISTICS

Date:

Time of day: AM/PM

Conditions:

Location:

Estimated distance: miles kilometres

Time (duration): hrs mins

Aims:

TRAINING TIP

Forewarned is forearmed. With the race route in mind (if you haven't run it, try to visualise it from a map) "think" your way around the course. How will you feel at different points of the course? Is there any likely low point you can predict?

warm-up:

warm-down:

Other exercise today:

Run details:

Accompanied by:

Comments:

TUESDAY

Thought for the Day:
The smallet deed is better than the grandest intention
– Roger Nash Baldwin

STATISTICS

Date:

Time of day: AM/PM

Conditions:

Location:

Estimated distance: miles kilometres

Time (duration): hrs mins

Aims:

TRAINING TIP

Do you know what kit you will run in? If not, sort it out and wear-test it over the next few runs. If anything rubs (Shoes, shorts, vest) change it for a different one until every item feels comfortable.

warm-up:

warm-down:

Other exercise today:

Run details:

Accompanied by:

Comments:

WEEK 14

WEDNESDAY

Thought for the Day:
You must be the change you wish to see in the world
– Mahatma Gandhi

STATISTICS

Date:

Time of day: AM/PM

Conditions:

Location:

Estimated distance: miles kilometres

Time (duration): hrs mins

Aims:

TRAINING TIP

Try running laps of a park, picking up the marathon brand energy drink at the intervals at which you expect to drink – perhaps every two miles. See if you can handle this routine comfortably. If not, don't try to stick to it during the race.

warm-up:

warm-down:

Other exercise today:

Run details:

Accompanied by:

Comments:

THURSDAY

Thought for the Day:
Both tears and sweat are salty, but they render a different result.
Tears will get you sympathy; sweat will get you change
– Rev. Jesse Jackson

STATISTICS

Date:

Time of day: AM/PM

Conditions:

Location:

Estimated distance: miles kilometres

Time (duration): hrs mins

Aims:

TRAINING TIP

If you feel any twinges in training, don't just ignore them and hope they go away. Stop immediately. Stretch out the muscle gently to check its condition. If in any doubt, get treatment. The training is almost over now, and overdoing it is too easy.

warm-up:

warm-down:

Other exercise today:

Run details:

Accompanied by:

Comments:

WEEK 14

FRIDAY

Thought for the Day:
There is no such thing in anyone's life as an unimportant day
– Alexander Woollcott

STATISTICS

Date:

Time of day: AM/PM

Conditions:

Location:

Estimated distance: miles kilometres

Time (duration): hrs mins

Aims:

TRAINING TIP

Think through your arrangements for getting to the start of the race. If you have not yet booked accommodation needed, do so right away. You do not want last-minute unattended arrangements to get in the way of marathon performance.

warm-up:

warm-down:

Other exercise today:

Run details:

Accompanied by:

Comments:

SATURDAY

Thought for the Day:
If you think you can, you can. And if you think you can't, you're right
– Mary Kay Ash

STATISTICS

Date:

Time of day: AM/PM

Conditions:

Location:

Estimated distance: miles kilometres

Time (duration): hrs mins

Aims:

TRAINING TIP

Find a picture of the finishing line of the marathon you will run, or even visit the location. Imagine yourself coming across the finish line – what you would look like, and how you would feel. You should store this image for motivation during the race.

warm-up:

warm-down:

Other exercise today:

Run details:

Accompanied by:

Comments:

WEEK 14

WEEK 15

2 weeks to go

The pattern of all those preceding weeks continues – a long run and one other training session which you extend beyond your regular run. But the

end is near. You are now into the 'easing down' period, in which you are doing progressively less taxing training, in order to allow your body to recover more comprehensively from the training build-up to which you have subjected it in the last few weeks.

Many people find it difficult to reduce their efforts. They have been striving to complete training sessions and feel the achievement in doing so. The training has always been a means to an end though, and the end is now in sight. In the last two weeks extra training is not productive, it will merely tire you out and lead to under-performance on race day.

The "controlled efforts" suggested later in the week are more to allay unreasonable fears of 'losing fitness' than for any physiological boost. You may feel a need to run faster at some point to maintain your confidence. If so, contain your effort within a few sections of the run – no more than five minutes at a time, and no more than three or four of these, with equal time spent slowly jogging in between as a recovery. Use 15 minutes at either end of the run for warming up and warming down.

Suggested Routine

SUNDAY	Long run – 2 hours
MONDAY	recovery
TUESDAY	30 minutes running
WEDNESDAY	recovery
THURSDAY	1 hour running, keep faster running in short controlled efforts
FRIDAY	recovery
SATURDAY	recovery

WEEK 15

SUNDAY

Thought for the Day:
A hero is no braver than an ordinary man, but he is braver five minutes longer
– Ralph Waldo Emerson

STATISTICS

Date:

Time of day: AM/PM

Conditions:

Location:

Estimated distance: miles kilometres

Time (duration): hrs mins

Aims:

TRAINING TIP
In your last long run concentrate on feeling comfortable. Maybe your marathon will take twice as long, so make sure you finish the training feeling that you have something to spare.

warm-up:

warm-down:

Other exercise today:

Run details:

Accompanied by:

Comments:

MONDAY

Thought for the Day:
Respect yourself most of all
– Pythagoras

STATISTICS

Date:

Time of day: AM/PM

Conditions:

Location:

Estimated distance: miles kilometres

Time (duration): hrs mins

Aims:

TRAINING TIP

"Winding down", doing less running, could leave you feeling that you are missing something. Replace time you would have spent running with some other pleasurable activity. As long as it is not physically taxing, you will still be tapering your effort appropriately.

warm-up:

warm-down:

Other exercise today:

Run details:

Accompanied by:

Comments:

TUESDAY

Thought for the Day:
The ultimate measure of a man is not where he stands in moments of comfort and convenience, but where he stands at moments of challenge and controversy – Martin Luther King

STATISTICS

Date:

Time of day: AM/PM

Conditions:

Location:

Estimated distance: miles kilometres

Time (duration): hrs mins

Aims:

TRAINING TIP

Don't try to fight tiredness during a run. Just slow the pace and cover the ground. Allow your mind to wander so you are not continually thinking "how far to go?"

warm-up:

warm-down:

Other exercise today:

Run details:

Accompanied by:

Comments:

WEEK 15

WEDNESDAY

Thought for the Day:
You know more than you think you do
– Dr Spock

STATISTICS

Date:

Time of day: _____ AM/PM

Conditions:

Location:

Estimated distance: _____ miles _____ kilometres

Time (duration): _____ hrs _____ mins

Aims:

TRAINING TIP

Try to synchronise your day with the time at which the race will be held. On rest days make sure your timing is in tune with the possibility of starting to run at race time, by breakfasting well before then and stretching etc – unless your target race is very early of course!

warm-up:

warm-down:

Other exercise today:

Run details:

Accompanied by:

Comments:

THURSDAY

Thought for the Day:
I'm all ready you see. Now my troubles will have trouble with me
– Dr Seuss

STATISTICS

Date:

Time of day: _____ AM/PM

Conditions:

Location:

Estimated distance: _____ miles _____ kilometres

Time (duration): _____ hrs _____ mins

Aims:

TRAINING TIP

Be aware that your mind is playing games with you. If you feel unduly tired, this is probably because your brain is telling your body you have a big task ahead, and should save appointed energy until the appointed day.

warm-up:

warm-down:

Other exercise today:

Run details:

Accompanied by:

Comments:

WEEK 15

FRIDAY

Thought for the Day:
Less is more
– Mies van der Rohe

STATISTICS

Date:
Time of day: AM/PM
Conditions:

Location:
Estimated distance: miles kilometres
Time (duration): hrs mins

Aims:

TRAINING TIP
Rest becomes more important the closer you get to the race. You may have to force yourself to relax. Try to set aside an hour during the day when you can rest up, by reading the paper or watching TV.

warm-up:
warm-down:
Other exercise today:

Run details:

Accompanied by:

Comments:

SATURDAY

Thought for the Day:
Things do not change – we change
– Henry David Thoreau

STATISTICS

Date:
Time of day: AM/PM
Conditions:

Location:
Estimated distance: miles kilometres
Time (duration): hrs mins

Aims:

TRAINING TIP
With the deadline looming you may start to feel anxious about your likely performance. Divert yourself inot a more positive frame of mind by looking back rather than forward. Remember what it was like two or three months ago and how far you have come.

warm-up:
warm-down:
Other exercise today:

Run details:

Accompanied by:

Comments:

WEEK 15

WEEK 16

Marathon week

In the last couple of weeks before a marathon, you should be doing less running. Your body has been trained for the task over the last few months. To be ready for the big day, it needs to rest up a little. This is a delicate operation. Rest doesn't mean putting your feet up, it just means doing a little less than normal. It should be a gradual process. You should already have started to ease off over the penultimate week, and in the final week before the race you should do no more than half of what you have become used to during a normal week.

Suggested Routine

SUNDAY	Long run between 1 hour and 90 minutes
MONDAY	Recovery day
TUESDAY	30 minutes' running
WEDNESDAY	Rest day
THURSDAY	30 minutes' running
FRIDAY	Rest day
SATURDAY	Registration and rest day
SUNDAY	Marathon day

SUNDAY

Seven days to go

The long run a week before the race should be between one hour and 90 minutes. This should give you long enough on your feet to provide your body with a reminder of the long-run routine, but not so long as to tire yourself out. Concentrate on a steady pace and imagine that you are running the first part of next week's race, maybe up to a third of the distance. Make sure that you stay well within your capabilities, so that you finish still feeling fresh and ready for more.

MONDAY

Six days to go

This is a recovery day as normal after a long run – even though the long run was not nearly as long as those you will have previously tackled. You may not feel like you need to "recover" after such a modest effort. Take the opportunity to relax. It is something you need to learn, and to practise.

Resist any temptation to compensate for any part of the plan in these last few days. It's too late now for any effort in training to be effective during the marathon. The last few days are mainly an exercise in avoiding over-exertion and mishap. Take steps one at a time, literally: racing up them two at a time could strain a muscle. And don't dare run for that bus you were chasing a few months ago.

Read through the information you have been sent about procedures for registration, getting to the start on marathon morning, and any other advice offered by the marathon organisers. Surprisingly few people do this, yet it can save a lot of time and worry on marathon morning to know what has to be done at what time. You will be more in control of your circumstances than if you have to respond to unexpected requirements just before the marathon starts.

TUESDAY

Five days to go

There is less to do on the physical side of things. The reduction in training load may let all kind of psychological side-effects out of the bag. Am I doing enough? Should I run faster? Why does it feel just as hard to run at a slower pace as it did when I was running more last week?

The 30 minutes of running recommended are just to keep your muscles primed and your body ticking over in stand-by mode. It is not to enhance your capabilities even more for marathon day. You are doing enough, and you shouldn't run any faster. Why you may feel that the effort is just as much now as it was when you were doing a much greater level of training is a more complicated question. Your body is probably doing what it is supposed to do even while your mind is resisting the idea. Your body knows what is coming and is creating the conditions under which it can most effectively gather strength – that is, by resting. It sends out messages to your brain that it has had enough for the day, even though it may be a fraction of the work of which it is capable.

WEDNESDAY

Four days to go

This is a genuine rest day. You will not have done anything so strenuous the day before that you need to recover from it. You will be able to take 30 minutes' running in your stride and feel no after-effect. It is a very modest effort in relation to what you have done on previous days. But think back to what 30 minutes of running may have meant before you began the 16-week programme, or before you began to run regularly at all. It may well have been inconceivable that you could run so far, almost without noticing, yet it has come about. The marathon itself, once so distant a target, is now also within your grasp.

Without having to schedule any running for the day, you could set aside some time to deal with the nervousness which you may be feeling as you approach marathon day. Don't put this off until it starts to affect your sleep. Consider the doubts you may have, whether they could be more general concerns about life or specific worries about the marathon itself. Confront all such thoughts. Make a list of them and then worry your way intensively and creatively down the list. Each item will stimulate thoughts about why it is a source of worry. Think about what you can do to minimise and contain each one. Repeat this process, devoting a limited amount of time to each aspect. By doing so, you should be able to prevent nervousness welling up and overwhelming you. You can reduce your level of anxiety by familiarity and by a constructive attitude towards it.

THURSDAY

Three days to go

Start the day with your 30-minute run. If you wish to adjust your diet to increase your carbohydrate intake, now is the time to start this. Muscle glycogen (your source of readily available energy on race day) can be boosted by eating carbohydrate-rich foods over the final few days. Do not increase the amount of food you eat, just increase the proportion of it made up by complex carbohydrates, that is, starchy foods, like bread, potatoes, pasta and rice. Avoid fatty foods, and consume protein-rich foods, like meat or eggs, only

in small quantities. You can buy a proprietary "carbohydrate booster" in powdered form, which will allow you to increase your carbohydrate intake while minimising any "bloated" feeling. Many sports shops will sell this, packaged in a 500g drum, in a choice of flavours.

Glycogen is stored in the muscles with water, so you should also be consciously hydrating yourself. Drink water regularly, every hour or so, in normal quantities – a glass at a time. You will need the water both for storing glycogen and for ensuring that you get to the start line fully "topped up" with water. During the marathon you will not be able to replace water comfortably at the same rate that you sweat it out. Check your level of hydration by the colour of your urine. It should be a pale straw colour. Avoid "diuretics", such as tea, coffee, cola and alcohol, which will draw water out of your body.

There is a possibility of "over-hydration". This is when excessive water intake – and consequent outflow – flushes minerals out of your body. The solution is to take in minerals with the water. Drinking an occasional glass of fruit juice or eating a banana (also a good source of carbohydrate) every once in a while will achieve this.

FRIDAY

Two days to go

Unless you live locally to the venue of the marathon, this rest day will quite likely coincide with travelling there (see page 120 regarding marathons abroad). Avoid leaving home too early, or arriving at your destination too late. You need to make arrangements to allow for sleeping and eating at customary times. Try to avoid much change to your normal routine, or at least the basics of it. Travelling can be stressful,

Remind yourself of all the preparatory details of race morning. Decide when you will wake up, what and when you will eat. This may involve putting aside food the night before. You should know exactly how you will be getting to the start, and how long this will take. If you need to take a taxi, book it now. Decide how long any warm-up (including stretching) may take and decide when you will deposit your bag. Check the race instructions for lining up, as your race number may imply starting from a particular "pen". You may be unable to avoid standing at the start line quite a long time in advance of the start. Take an outer layer of clothing with you which you can discard during the marathon, as you begin to warm up. Arrange exactly where you will meet your friends or family after the marathon, and where they will be watching along the route.

Eat a carbohydrate-rich evening meal, and avoid alcohol. Set your alarm, or request an alarm call for the time you have planned, several hours before the start of the marathon. Do not go to bed unrealistically early. If you lie awake for very long this may contribute to nervousness. Even if you cannot sleep, just close your eyes and relax as completely as you can. The amount of sleep you have the night before a marathon will not influence your performance much, as long as you do not spend the night worrying about it.

and this can burn nervous energy. Avoid unfamiliar situations, concentrating hard, or getting bored. Try to remain calm if you encounter difficulties, and stay focused on your immediate aims, which are to eat normally, arrive at your destination in a state of calm, and get a good night's sleep.

SATURDAY

One day to go

Most marathons will require you to register within a few days of the race. If you are local you can do this earlier in the week and avoid crowds at the marathon expo where race registration normally takes place. If you have to register on the Saturday, do so as early as practicable without cutting short your night's sleep. Do not stay too long at the race expo. Spending time on your feet, talking a lot and negotiating your way slowly through crowds are sure ways to tire yourself out. Collect your race number and your chip (if the chip timing system is being used) and get away again promptly.

It is not productive to run the day before a marathon unless you find that it provides a means of relaxing nerves. If you do run, just jog gently for no more than 20 minutes. Fix your number to whatever top you will be wearing during the marathon and secure your chip to your shoelaces. If you lose either of these before the start, you will not be able to do the race.

SUNDAY

Marathon Day

The first thing to do after getting out of bed is to eat a light breakfast, which you will be able to digest before the start. This would probably consist of toast, juice or water – and a(nother) banana. Do not eat a cooked breakfast, even if this is included in the price of your accommodation. Use the toilet before you leave for the start. The toilet facilities at the start will be in great demand.

You should be prepared to hang around a lot. Stick to your pre-arranged schedule for stowing baggage and lining up. Use toilets as necessary, but be on the lookout for those further away which may have shorter queues. Stop drinking water about 90 minutes before the start and empty your bladder as late as possible before lining up at the start. Avoid any sugary drinks until you have started to run. Your warm-up can be limited to incidental jogging (to and from the toilet, perhaps) and some careful stretches (perhaps while already lined up).

It will probably be very crowded in the early stages of the race. Do not strive to overtake. If necessary, resign yourself to a slightly slower pace than you anticipated and wait until the field thins out enough for you to overtake without dodging and weaving between others. The best strategy is to conserve energy. You will be able to make up time you lose in the early

WEEK 16

stages by remaining in better shape for longer towards the end of the marathon.

Take drinks from early on in the race, little and often. When you come to a drink station, do not stop to pick up the first cup or bottle you see. The drink station will occupy several tables, each separated by several metres, and further along it is likely to be less crowded. If you have not practised drinking on the move, stop for a second or two. When drinking "energy replacement" drinks from open cups this avoids spillage and the unpleasant stickiness it can cause. Discard your cup or bottle carefully, and watch out for debris underfoot where other runners have been less considerate.

Divide the marathon into phases in which you can focus on one particular objective at a time. The phases you choose will depend on the nature of the course, and perhaps where you expect to see people you know, but in the early stages your objective will be to expend the least energy in tackling them. Make the last phase, when you will be counting down the distance to go, as short as possible.

Afterwards

When you cross the finish line, remember to look up (don't check your wristwatch) and strike a pose appropriate for your souvenir finish photograph – whether you intend to buy one or not. Slow to a walk but keep moving through as others come in behind you. Pause for the race officials to remove your timing chip. Accept your finisher's medal and goody bag, and whatever else race helpers are there to provide. Your baggage will be stored according to your race number, so look for the signs directing you to the appropriate place. You

probably need not remember to do any of this, as race officials are there to process you as smoothly as possible with little or no effort necessary on your part. Only when you exit the finish area do you become your own master again. At that point, try not to crumple into a heap. Put on some warm clothing, if you have not already done so. Drink water or energy drinks to re-hydrate. Eat light snack food (some will be provided in your finisher bag). Make your way to where you have arranged to meet family or friends, or else keep moving away to pick up public transport home.

Hanging around, taking in the atmosphere and basking in your achievement may be more appealing than scurrying home, but be aware that if you stop still in any one place for very long, it may become very hard to get moving again.

This will continue to be the case for the next 48 hours. You can alleviate the after-effects by getting a massage, stretching gently and frequently, and walking as much as possible.

But you may prefer to revel masochistically in the after-effects. Walk backwards downstairs to show you've done the race. Take time off work. Or drag yourself into work and proudly sport your medal. Do whatever you want – you have achieved something and deserve to enjoy the feeling of accomplishment.

How was it for you?

Don't run. Leave at least a week before you start running again, and when you do, avoid racing for a month, then see how you feel. In retrospect, did you enjoy it?

Wanna do it again?

WEEK 16

7
Nutrition

You are what you eat, so becoming a marathon runner will change your diet. This is almost inevitable, which means that you don't have much choice in the matter. Mostly, it just happens naturally.

If you are used to the "see food" diet – eating what you want, and not worrying about it – then marathon running will not change that habit. It's just your wants that may change, stimulated by the new demands you are placing on your body.

There is a bit more to marathon nutrition than just saying "yes" to your belly, but it's unlikely that you will have to do more than concentrate on a few key points. For the rest of it, your body will make the decisions for you.

A marathon runner's diet has to fuel the muscles so that the body can cover the distances required in training. It has to replace the fluid that is sweated out while doing so. And it has to supply the vitamins and minerals that everyone needs, but which marathon runners will miss more immediately.

Carbohydrate, Fats and Protein

Running burns glycogen, which is stored carbohydrate. Because only limited amounts can be stored in the muscles, glycogen needs replacing after training or racing. This isn't complicated: shortly after running your body will crave carbohydrate. In other words, you will feel hungry and the kind of food you will want will be that most easily digested. If you do finish a long run with an appetite for a juicy steak, it is probably more to do with it being a tasty accompaniment to a mountain of potatoes.

Pasta is the runner's favourite form of carbohydrate. There is a very good reason for this: it's easy to cook. When you come home tired and hungry, it's hard to heave yourself out of the nearest armchair, never mind start slaving away in the kitchen. Pasta just needs emptying into a saucepan and boiling up for a few minutes. For flavour just slop in a bit of bottled sauce and stir. By this time you may find it hard work just to raise the fork to your mouth and chew. To do so may be an effort, but the revitalising effects slowly become apparent.

One international runner, describing this process after particularly hard training sessions, called it "coming back to life again". An uninitiated observer, witnessing this ritual, admitted: "there's more to this running thing than meets the eye".

The usual dietary advice is to avoid fat and large amounts of protein. This is because these categories are usually consumed in far greater quantities than the body requires. Convenience foods are often dripping in fat: burgers, chips, crisps, doughnuts. It is this kind of food that a runner can especially do without. The fats and proteins quickly give an uncomfortably stuffed feeling, which makes it unlikely that you will want to run for hours afterwards. Carbohydrates – much more easily digested – can fill the gap left by eating less fatty or protein-rich foods without prejudice to your exercise regime.

You should also try to avoid sugary foods, especially before you run. In moderation, after you have completed your run, these are fine. At other times stick to "complex" carbohydrates – starchy foods – and avoid added sugar. This will minimise the fluctuations in your blood sugar levels. After running is also the time to use any of the brand "energy replacement drinks", if you wish to do so. In fact, there is little these somewhat expensive products can do for you that ordinary fruit juice can't. Do not use them before running.

It is unlikely that you will have to make any great effort to change your eating habits when you take up running. If you run regularly, this will itself change your preferences in such a way that your eating habits become more compatible with your exercise habits.

Water, alcohol and caffeine

Carbohydrate is stored in the muscles as glycogen. Water is required to do this. The single most beneficial change runners can make to their diet is probably to increase their intake of water. Most of us consume water in some other form, and some of these forms, like alcohol and coffee, actually result in a net outflow of water. In the process of their excretion, alcohol and caffeine draw water out of the body. Runners may need to reduce their consumption of these and other

CARBO-BOOSTING

The easiest way to increase carbo-hydrate intake is to mix "carbo-booster" powder with water and consume it as a drink. The unflavoured variety is inoffensive to the taste.

"diuretics", or else significantly boost their water consumption to compensate.

Vitamins and minerals

In the form of fruit or fruit juice, water intake can also provide the vitamins and minerals required by the body. A large through flow of water by itself may otherwise flush out these essential nutrients. Another conscious change you may need to make to your diet is to increase the amount of fruit you eat. If you eat a balanced diet, you shouldn't need to take vitamin pills or other supplements, but you may find some psychological value in doing so. If so, a basic, cheap multivitamin pill is enough.

When to eat

When you feel hungry, of course. But when you feel hungry will depend a lot on when you run.

Breakfast

If you do your run first thing in the morning, you may not want to eat beforehand. To reduce unnecessary strain on your body, try to avoid going from sleeping to running in less than half an hour. Use the first part of that half hour to drink a glass of water and eat a slice of bread, or a cup of (weak) tea and a slice of toast. Anything spread on the toast should be spread very sparingly. Then do some gentle warming up before you start your run. When you finish, take your real breakfast. Cereal, toast, and orange juice are all things that you can eat immediately. If you run to work, it may take a little more ingenuity to come up with a post-run breakfast that is both easy and satisfying. Try not to substitute coffee and pastries for a proper meal.

Lunch

If you do a lunchtime run, don't miss lunch. To fit a run, a shower and lunch into a "lunch hour" may be asking too much. If you can't take extra time at lunch, perhaps you should avoid running then. If you can fit it in, make sure that you have prepared sandwiches for afterwards.

Evening meal

If you run in the afternoon or evening, you may be able to follow your run with your evening meal. If you finish your run some time before your meal, have a light snack immediately afterwards so that your muscles can refuel while they are most receptive to doing so.

Motivational meals

Rules are there to be broken. If breaking them can motivate you, then harness this as a "reward" following particular training sessions. During a long run, I often dream of the leisurely breakfast of bacon, eggs and coffee that will follow.

BREAKFAST OF CHAMPS: YOU CAN INDULGE YOURSELF AFTER A LONG RUN.

8
Common Problems

The best-laid plans unfailingly go awry. The precise form problems may take is impossible to predict, but here are some of those regularly encountered on the journey to the marathon start line.

You will meet with distinctive kinds of problems. These will fall into two basic categories: administrative and physical. The administrative problems – how to enter races and to find out what is required of you as a participant, for example – will have definite answers. The physical problems – those concerning injury – are not usually so amenable to such clear-cut solutions. There are an infinite number of problems that may arise under either heading. Some examples of each appear below. For those questions for which there is a definite answer, the challenge is to identify the source from which it may be obtained. Some useful sources of further information are listed in the following chapter.

For questions where there is no definite answer immediately available – particularly those concerning injury – you must remain the ultimate judge. Don't place your faith in any received answer, until you have applied your own judgement to the evidence. Draw out evidence from whatever source you can. For example, massage treatment is not always the answer, but it almost always tells you more about the injury and helps to indicate what other treatment may be appropriate. In any situation you need to "feel out" your condition, by whatever means, before determining action.

TAKING UP RUNNING

Q I have started to follow a 16-week marathon programme, but I often have to fly abroad for business and because of my schedules it is difficult to fit in the training. I've got a week's trip coming up when it will be difficult for me to fit any running in, so I wonder what I can do to get back on track with the schedule when I come back. Any tips?

A Whether you are unable to fulfil the schedule through other commitments, or through injury, do not attempt to "catch up" on "lost" training by doing more than usual. This is a certain way to become injured. Just continue with the schedule from the point you have reached.

Q I have just reached retirement age and I'd like to take up running. Is there anything I should be careful of at my age?

A Taking up running at retirement age, 60–65, is late in life, especially if you have not recently been very active. There is a risk that you may have hitherto undiagnosed heart disease. Get a medical checkup and a good pair of shoes. Go for brisk walks and intersperse walking with gentle jogging, even more gradually than suggested in the early chapters of this book. If you get tightness or pain in the chest, or sudden shortness of breath or faintness, STOP. Seek medical advice before progressing your running. If you have not run for many years, you are likely to get biomechanical problems unless you progress very slowly.*

INITIAL HICCUPS

Q I've just started to run again after a very long time and am getting shin splints each time I have run for a little while – how can I overcome this?

A Starting to run can be a strain on the body – and the signs of strain may appear in particular parts of it. You should be careful to only gradually introduce any new activity, particularly a repetitive action like running. Shin splints (inflammation of the tibial and toe extensor muscles), and other muscular problems and aches and pains may be a sign that you have overdone things. You need to reduce the strain, and can do this in several different ways. You could run less often, or less far – in acute cases you may have to stop running entirely for a while. Or you can try to run on soft surfaces like grass instead of hard pavements, or you could try using heel pads to help absorb the shock transmitted through your legs every time your foot strikes the ground. Make sure you have more than one pair of running shoes at any one time, and change from one pair to the other from time to time. All this will help to reduce or diffuse the strain, which is the root cause of the problem. For symptomatic relief, you may need to consult a physiotherapist.

Q I have been running for a little while now and feel that I can already see an improvement in my fitness and timings, but now a friend of mine would like to join me and she will be starting from scratch. I don't want to deter her, but how can we accommodate our different levels of fitness and still run together? I don't want to slip backwards!

A Now you have been running for some time you may have progressed to the position where you modulate your training according to a hard day/easy day pattern. In other words, you no longer rest completely between alternate training days, but simply take things easier on your "rest" days, continuing to run. This suggests that when you train with someone slower than you are, you should do so on your "easy" days, when you will be running slower, and probably for less time/distance.

Even on your hard training days, there will be scope to accommodate company. You need to warm up and warm down at each end of your training session at a gentle pace. If you are repeating efforts in your training, it is likely that you will do so on a lap course. Perhaps your friend could try this sort of training by accompanying you for every second effort, or the first part of every effort, or complete a smaller loop in the same time as you run a larger one.

Company is particularly valuable on long runs. If you do these runs as repeated laps, having someone join you for a lap or two in the middle or towards the end can make time and distance pass while hardly noticing the effort involved. It is a different story if you have nothing to concentrate on other than your own increasing fatigue and discomfort.

Q I think I may have pulled my calf muscle. How long does it take on average to get over something like this? I tried running after about a week's rest and although it seemed OK at first, it felt tight and painful a little while after I finished my run.

A How well you recover depends very much on your age. Muscle strains that heal within a few days in your twenties may take weeks for someone in their fifties. The crucial thing is to stop running the instant that you sense there is a problem. This may involve an embarrassing and chilly walk home from wherever you have got to, but it is far better than sustaining more serious damage. If you do this, then ice the affected muscle as soon as you can to contain the internal bleeding and swelling that results when muscle fibres tear. Use a stretch bandage to compress the tissues immediately surrounding the area, and, if possible, elevate your leg so that blood does not collect in the damaged area. This course of action – rest, ice, compression and elevation (RICE) may be enough to dispel symptoms very quickly.

If you run before the symptoms disappear, then they are likely to revisit you. After the first 24 hours you may also benefit from massage to the affected area (see page 123 in Further information). You will have to use your own judgement as to when to resume training.

This may only be possible to determine by trial and error. See how it feels in the first few hundred metres of your run, and be fully prepared to stop at the first sign that the old problem is still there.

Q My friend has just discovered that she is pregnant and is a regular runner. What adjustments should she make to her running schedule, if any, and how soon after she has had the baby (assuming there are no complications), can she begin running again?

A Running during pregnancy needs some discretion. The amount you can safely run depends on how much you were doing before. If all is going well you will put on a significant amount of weight (approximately 10kg/22lb). Your ligaments become more lax and you should be careful on uneven surfaces as your centre of gravity moves forwards and you may trip or fall. Long runs on a hot day may be hazardous for your baby, as your body temperature rises.

If you jog regularly until the last three or four weeks of pregnancy, you will keep fitter and probably have an easier labour, but you must let the pregnancy dictate what you do and follow the advice of your obstetrician.

Following pregnancy the body takes time to readjust, and, if you are breast feeding, it is important not to get too dehydrated and to eat adequately. Take your time returning to full training.*

Q I am diabetic, how should I adjust my intake of carbohydrates before a race or should I be taking any extra precautions regarding my food intake?

A The diabetes question is complicated. What you should do will depend on the type and severity of the diabetes you have, your diet, how many doses of insulin you require, your blood glucose level etc. You should take advice from your own doctor.*

Q I'm getting a pain along the bottom of my foot, sort of underneath the instep, when I run. What's the most likely cause and

what kind of treatment do I need?

A You need to consult a podiatrist, and maybe get a biomechanical assessment. This will seek to determine if your running gait is creating specific problems for your feet, and what might be done to alleviate such problems by exercising more control over the motion of the foot as it strikes the ground.

You may be able to do this by selecting a certain type of shoe (in which case a podiatrist will be able to advise you). If this is not sufficiently corrective, then you can be prescribed orthotics. These are moulded specifically to the shape of your foot, and are inserted into the shoe either in place of, or on top of, the standard shoe insole.

Q My doctor says I have bunions. Are there any special running shoes to cope with this problem?

A Some brands of shoes are available in width fittings, and this may help to accommodate your foot more comfortably, but the width of the shoe is not the only criterion you may need to consider. Ideally, you should consult a podiatrist before you buy any running-specific footwear.

Q My teenage daughter has taken up running in order to do a marathon, but I am worried she is over-training. How would I recognise if this were the case?

A Over-training may increase susceptibility to recurrent infections. If the training load is too great, the level of performance will begin to deteriorate. Your daughter must recognise this for what it is, and not ignore it or explain away a loss of form by other factors. It is likely she will suffer feelings of fatigue and depression. The resting heart rate will increase (the complete opposite effect to when the stress-recovery cycle of training is in balance). She may also find that her periods stop.*

ORGANISING YOUR RACE

Q I don't want to go into a marathon without having tried a small race beforehand. How many races do you recommend a person enter before they try a marathon, or doesn't it matter?

A This is purely a matter of personal choice. It is not necessary to participate in any races before doing your first marathon, but it is often very helpful. Even though a marathon is very different from other races, familiarising yourself with a race situation will be of great help. You will get to know what to do before the start (see page 108 Marathon week) and will reduce nervousness when marathon time comes. Select shorter races: maybe try a 10km to start and then a half marathon. Pick a big race to get the feel of a significant occasion. Otherwise, do races when you want and select those which appeal to you.

Q I've decided I'd like to run a marathon, but I want to combine it with a little holiday afterwards. How easy is it to register for a marathon in a different country? Do they favour local people in choosing from applicants?

A Most races favour overseas runners. They bring more cash into the local economy, which is often of direct benefit to race sponsors. Many races are set up specifically in order to attract tourist runners and will make it easy to enter, although this may have to be done by a particular date, after which entries will be closed. Most international races allow for online entries through their website. Sometimes race entry fees increase as the race date approaches.

Registration is a separate, further step and is most often required at the race venue (large races often register runners at a marathon expo). This is where you will actually receive your race number (if it has not been sent through

the post) and have your timing "chip" primed for the particular race timing system (if the race uses such a system, which is increasingly the case).

Some races operate a qualifying limit whereby all competitors must have previously recorded certain times for the marathon. Boston is the most well known of these. Others, like London and New York, are heavily over-subscribed and allocate only limited places to overseas runners. Most often, as a foreign runner, you can get an entry into these races if you buy a travel-and-accommodation package through one of the race's official tour operators, but this can be expensive. Overseas runners seeking places independent of such an arrangement are selected through a lottery system, and the chances of success are often not very good.

Q If I wish to run a marathon abroad, will I need to produce any evidence of my fitness to enter? Where are the rules most stringent?

A Most often you will only be asked to sign a basic disclaimer on the race entry form, agreeing that you are doing the race at your own risk. In some countries, particularly France and Italy, there is a further requirement that you supply a doctor's certificate that you are deemed fit to run a marathon (or any race) before you will be given a race number. This kind of certificate should be obtainable from your local GP, but there will probably be a charge – and this can vary. You need only go for the most basic form of examination and testimony at the cheapest rate to satisfy the requirements of the race organisers, who themselves are acting under this rule enacted by their national athletic federations – they have not themselves chosen to impose it. Their own nationals need only quote their registration number to be exempted from this requirement. Foreign runners may be able to quote a similar number, although

in Britain the only likely number you can use may be on the membership card of your running club. The club in turn is affiliated to the athletic federation, and a copy of this document proving that the club exists may also be useful.

Q I am running in a marathon abroad and it will mean a long flight to get there. How much time should I allow to recover from my flight and complete my registration etc?

A There are two factors at work here: the length of the flight and the number of hours' time change. A rule of thumb is to allow one day for each hour of time change. North-south journeys, where there is little or no time change, still require recovery, and may complicate the question by also requiring a significant climatic adjustment. If you go to the tropics from temperate latitudes, then you should allow 8–14 days for acclimatisation to the heat. In other words, it is better to do the race towards the end of your stay. Even if there is no climatic change and no time change, you should still allow a couple of days to recover from the journey. Do not run immediately after arrival, but ease yourself into your new surroundings first, maybe with a swim or a massage. You will also need to make sure you re-hydrate from the drying effect of a long-haul flight before you run.

RACE PRACTICALITIES

Q Where do you leave your things before you start a marathon? Do the organisers provide a kind of "open air" cloakroom for runners?

A Small races may not provide any "left luggage" facility, and you may have to lock belongings in your car and run with the keys, or make other arrangements. Most races will have a secure area within which you can leave bags, but when the race is point-to-point they must be transported to the finish.

When this happens it is important that you use the bag supplied by the race organisation. This may be transparent, or it may have your race number fixed to it for easy identification by the personnel who retrieve it at the race finish. If you do not reclaim your bag at the finish, make sure you contact the race organisation as soon as possible afterwards. They will probably have it sitting in their office awaiting your appearance.

Q I have friends who will be meeting me (hopefully!) at the end of the marathon that I'm running in. Obviously they can't meet me at the finish line, but what rules are there generally about friends and family keeping away from the start and finish areas of marathons?

A There are no fixed rules, other than that non-runners must not cross the finish line. Even then, in smaller races, a young child accompanying their parent through the finish may be tolerated. Bigger races will have their own security, which will leave you in little doubt if you are encroaching on the race organisation's territory. In such cases, you would meet your friends in the "reunion" area, where the restricted finish area feeds into unrestricted public space. There are quite likely to be posts or trees nearby with letters attached to them in order to assist runners and their supporters in identifying a meeting place. Do not rely on contacting each other by mobile phone. The density of phone traffic at race finishes often causes the system to crash.

Q I like running with my portable CD player so I can listen to music. Is this allowed in an official race?

A Yes. Many fancy-dress participants in the London Marathon, for example, carry articles far more cumbersome than a CD player. As long as

you do not present a hazard to other runners, like entangling them in your wires, you should be OK.

Q I've read recently about the use of pacesetters in marathons and I wondered how this works in practice. Do they have to enter the race officially as well?

A Competent pacemakers offer a very useful service to race organisers, helping them get the most out of their star athletes, who are themselves invited to participate at great expense. Organisers are prepared to pay pacemakers a good fee, subject to guarantees of a particular specified pace. They nonetheless do have to be officially entered into the race. This will be done by the race organisation, as it is on behalf of all the top runners. These runners will be handed their start number and timing chip, and taken to the start line.

There are remarkably few rules which apply in road racing, and it cannot be assumed that track rules are transferable to road racing. Pacing on the track goes on despite rules discouraging it, but there are well-defined rules on what constitutes "assistance". Any runner receiving assistance, such as accepting drinks passed by another runner, renders themselves liable to disqualification. In road races this is impossible to police throughout the entire field, but a race referee will travel in a vehicle at the head of the race to observe the leading runners, and is able to disqualify runners observed transgressing rules.

In most road races women are mixed in among the men, which means that men are able to pace women to faster times, right to the end of the race. Typically, when men pace men or women pace women, the pacemaking does not go beyond 25km or at most 30km (15–20 miles). There has been much discussion about women's road

records being recognised specifically for women-only races, but to date the world governing body of athletics, the International Association of Athletic Federations, accepts times set in mixed races where women can benefit from male pacemakers right through to the finish line.

COPING WITH PROBLEMS DURING A MARATHON

Q I'm a little worried about running with so many other people in a marathon, when all I've done is a few smaller races. If I get injured, what sort of help is available along a normal marathon route?

A You are right to be concerned, but the major marathons usually have more effective delivery of medical assistance along the route than smaller events with less resources at their disposal. Increased numbers of runners, apart from generating a comprehensive programme of medical assistance – from a supply of Vaseline to on-course defibrillators – can increase the physical hazards faced by mid-pack runners.

The use of chip timing, which allows runners to see what time elapsed from when they crossed the start line to when they crossed the finish line (instead of from the firing of the start gun), has significantly reduced jostling to get away quickly at the start. Even so, in the early stages the road will be very crowded. You should not dodge your way forward. Apart from presenting a hazard to others, it is a wasteful use of energy. Crowd-control barriers will hold back spectators in particularly crowded places, or where the course narrows, but you should watch out for the "feet" of these barriers, which are not always positioned on the spectator side and can cause you to trip. Beware at water stations, too, where many people will verge to one side or the other, cutting in front of you. If you need to take a drink, do not stop at the first one offered – each station will have many tables from which to pick up a bottle or cup, and the further ones will probably be less crowded. You should also be careful to avoid tripping on discarded bottles and cups underfoot.

Q Someone recommended taking Ibuprofen before a race to help with any swelling in your leg joints. Is this a good idea?

A Ibuprofen can cause gastro-intestinal haemorrhage, which is more common in runners in endurance events. This increases the risk of vomiting blood. It cannot therefore be medically endorsed. If your joints swell when running you should not really be running – as you may sustain long-term damage.*

Q A friend of mine mentioned something about "hitting the wall" in a marathon – what is this and how do you overcome it?

A "Hitting the Wall" is an expression describing the feeling of debility that some runners suffer after 30–40km (18–25 miles) of a marathon. By no means all runners "hit the wall". Whether you do so or not is largely a matter of preparation.

Loading yourself up with carbo-hydrate in a big pasta dinner the night before the race is one way of trying to maximise the readily available energy stores that will be available for your body to draw upon during the race. Before the race, you should take in "complex carbohydrate" like pasta, rice, potatoes and bread – starchy foods – along with water. By doing this your body will store as much carbohydrate as possible as glycogen in the muscles. If you take energy drinks during the race (not before), you may also be able to take advantage of the simple sugars they contain so that your body burns up muscle glycogen more sparingly.

Despite these precautions, your muscles will probably run out of readily available energy during the later stages of a marathon. What happens next depends upon your conditioning. If you have become used to doing long runs, you will find that the changeover from using muscle glycogen to burning body fat is a seamless process. You will probably start to feel more tired, but this happens gradually. If you have not done any really long runs, then you may find that, as your body runs out of stored carbohydrate, you suddenly feel completely drained of energy. If this happens, do not fight against it. Slow down or even walk for a while. It is quite likely that you will feel better once your body has had time to adjust to obtaining energy through a different metabolic route.

Q Do you know any good (and quick!) remedies for blisters?

A Blisters are usually only a problem after a race. You may be aware they are forming during it, but as long as you don't stop running and then try to start again, you should be able to get to the finish before they become too painful. It is afterwards that you may start to hobble. Pierce the blister with a sterile needle, taking care only to touch the dead skin of the blister's surface. You may have to do this several times, in several places before the fluid completely drains from the blister. Doing this may be enough in itself, but if not you could then apply a proprietary dressing such as "second skin", or Compeed. This will protect the raw skin and allow it to grow underneath the dressing. To reduce the chances of getting blisters in the first place, use double-layer socks.

Q What is the simplest and most effective way to cure chafing – and to avoid the problem in the future?

A It is relatively easy to prevent "jogger's nipple", by taping over

them. In the groin area, things may be more problematic. Try out different kinds of shorts – with or without built-in briefs, looser fitting ones, or ones made of stretch lycra – to see if one kind suits you better. If you experience chafing during a race, then all that may be at hand are race marshals brandishing dollops of Vaseline. This may provide you with some relief.

RUNNING IN THE LONG TERM

Q I have just completed a half-marathon, and a friend of mine asked if I belonged to a club, but I don't know where I would find out about running clubs and I'm also unsure as to what I would get out of them. Will the club expect me to be at a certain fitness level and how will I know if it is a good one or not? Also, do they charge fees for joining, like a fitness club?

A Running clubs are many and varied. They will all charge membership fees, but at nothing like the same levels as fitness clubs. The charge will almost certainly be less than £50 ($75) per year. For this you will have an away-from-home venue from which to train and a varied calendar of races in which to compete, should you feel inclined to do so. You will meet many more people local to your area, who may be possible running partners. Most clubs welcome all levels of ability and you can select which races to compete in (if any) according to the level of competition you seek. To find out about clubs, contact the relevant regional Athletic Association (see page 123) who will have lists for their area. Otherwise, simply go to your local athletic track and ask there about which clubs use the facility. Most tracks are training venues for at least one running club, and sometimes several.

Medical advice above (indicated *) was kindly provided by Dr Dan Tunstall Pedoe, D Phil, FRCP (Medical Director of the London Marathon).

Further Information

These days you can run a marathon almost anywhere in the world – here is an extensive list of races from the Sahara to Antarctica, plus some organisations and websites to help you get on the right track.

GENERAL WEBSITES

www.runnersworld.co.uk
The best general website for runners in Britain

www.runnersworld.com
The best website for runners in the US

www.athle.com
The website of the French Athletic Federation

www.aims-association.org
The Association of International Marathons, providing information on 170 member events in 65 countries worldwide (including those overseas races listed below)

BRITISH RACES

ABINGDON MARATHON
www.abingdonamblers.co.uk
BATH HALF MARATHON
01225 471282
www.bathhalfmarathon.org.co.uk
BELFAST MARATHON
028 9027 3045
www.belfastcity.gov.uk
BLACKPOOL MARATHON
www.bpoolmarathon@aol.com
BRITISH OPEN 10KM (LONDON)
020 8569 7046
www.british10krunslondon.org
BUPA BRISTOL HALF MARATHON

0117 92 32148
CARDIFF MARATHON
012920 493387
CORNISH MARATHON
01579 362522
DUCHY MARATHON, CORNWALL
001736 366319
EDINBURGH MARATHON
09010 201600
www.edinburgh-marathon.co.uk
FLEET HALF MARATHON
www.fleethalfmarathon.com
FLORA LONDON HALF MARATHON
020 76204117
www.london-marathon.co.uk
FLORA LONDON MARATHON
020 7620 4117
www.london-marathon.co.uk
FOREST OF DEAN HALF MARATHON
01594 836408
www.fodac.org.uk
GREAT LANGDALE MARATHON
015395 61798
GREAT NORTH RUN
0191 456 2251
www.onrunning.com
GREAT SCOTTISH RUN (GLASGOW)
0141-248 9909
www.run.glasgow.gov.uk
HALSTEAD MARATHON (ESSEX)
01787 475780
www.halsteadmarathon.co.uk
HASTINGS HALF MARATHON
www.hastings-half.co.uk
ISLE OF MAN MARATHON
01624 842477
www.woodheights.freeserve.co.uk

ISLE OF WIGHT MARATHON
01983 616497
KINGSTON MARATHON
020 8399 3579
www.humanrace.co.uk
LEEDS MARATHON
0113 395 0001
LEICESTER MARATHON
0116 269 8786
www.leicestermarathon.org.uk
LIVERPOOL HALF MARATHON
www.runliverpool.org.uk
LOCH NESS MARATHON
0131 524 0360
www.lochnessmarathon.com
MORAY MARATHON
01343 54373
NEOLITHIC MARATHON
01380 725670
www.wiltshirewildlife.org
NEW FOREST MARATHON
01425 618180
www.nfma.org.uk
PETERBOROUGH HALF MARATHON
02476 431 942
www.peterbroughhalfmarathon.org
POTTERIES MARATHON
07760 218809
READING HALF MARATHON
020 8569 7046
www.readinghalmarathon.co.uk
ROBIN HOOD MARATHON (NOTTM)
020 8758 044
www.robinhoodmarathon.co.uk
ROTTINGDEAN MARATHON
01273 305000
www.windmillwalk.co.uk

SHAKESPEARE MARATHON
01789 550440
www.shakespearemarathon.org.uk
SNOWDONIA MARATHON
01492 860123
www.snowdonia-marathon.org.uk
ST ALBANS HALF MARATHON
01727 811084
THANET COASTAL MARATHON
01843 871169
www.thanetroadrunners.
freeserve.co.uk
TRESCO MARATHON (SCILLY IS)
01720 424106
www.tresco.co.uk
WOLVERHAMPTON MARATHON
07760 218809

For a listing of over 2000 UK running events check Rundown Events, published annually in February (2003 price £8.50) by GM Tippins, 62 Exe Vale Road, Exeter EX2 6LF

EUROPEAN RACES

AUSTRIA
VIENNA CITY MARATHON
00 43 1 606 9510
www.vienna-marathon.com

CROATIA
ZAGREB MARATHON
00 385 1 3650 543

CZECH REPUBLIC
PRAGUE MARATHON
00420 224 919 209
www.pim.cz

DENMARK
COPENHAGEN MARATHON
00 45 3526 6900
www.sparta.dk

ESTONIA
TALLINN MARATHON
00 372 641 4260
www.hot.ee/tallinnmarathon

FINLAND
HELSINKI CITY MARATHON
00 358 9 3481 2405
www.sul.fi

FRANCE
MARATHON DE MARSEILLE
00 33 4 91 48 45 17
www.marseillemarathon.com
MARATHON DU MEDOC
00 33 5 56 59 01 91
www.marathondumedoc.com
MARSEILLE-CASSIS CLASSIC
00 33 4 91 75 24 24
www.marseille-cassis.com
PARIS MARATHON
00 33 1 41 33 15 68
www.parismarathon.com

GERMANY
BERLIN 25KM
00 49 30 305 1771
www.25kmvonberlin.de
BERLIN MARATHON
00 49 30 301 288 10
www.berlin-marathon.com
OLYMPUS MARATHON HAMBURG
00 49 40 8888 0340
www.olympus-marathon-
hamburg.com

GREECE
ATHENS CLASSIC MARATHON
00 30 10 935 6905
www.athensclassicmarathon.gr

HUNGARY
BUDAPEST MARATHON
00 36 1 273 0939
www.budapestmarathon.com

ICELAND
REYKJAVIK MARATHON
00 354 588 3399
www.reykjavikmarathon.com

IRELAND
DUBLIN MARATHON
00 353 1 623 2250
www.dublincitymarathon.ie

ISRAEL
TIBERIAS MARATHON
00 972 3 648 6256

ITALY
FIRENZE MARATHON
00 390 55 600 664
www.firenzemarathon.it
ROME MARATHON
00 390 6 40 65 064
www.maratonadiroma.it
TURIN MARATHON
00 390 11 663 1231
www.turinmarathon.it
VENICE MARATHON
00 390 41 940 664
www.venicemarathon.it

LEBANON
BEIRUT MARATHON
00 961 3 359 259
www.beirutmarathon.org

LUXEMBOURG
ROUTE DU VIN HALF MARATHON
00 352 48 06 70
www.fla.lu

MALTA
MALTA CHALLENGE MARATHON
(3 days stage race)
00 356 21 34 43 78
www.maltachallengemarathon.com

MONACO
MONACO MARATHON
00 377 92 05 43 05
www.monaco-marathon.com

NETHERLANDS
AMSTERDAM MARATHON
00 31 20 663 0781
www.amsterdammarathon.nl
CITY-PIER-CITY HALF MARATHON
00 31 174 540 607
www.cpcloop.nl
ROTTERDAM MARATHON
00 31 10 291 9230
www.rotterdammarathon.nl

NORWAY
MIDNIGHT SUN MARATHON (TROMSO)
00 47 776 73363
www.msm.no

POLAND
WROCLAW MARATHON
00 48 71 354 81 69
www.mw.com.pl

PORTUGAL
LISBON HALF MARATHON
www.meiamaratonadelisboa.com

ROMANIA
BUCHAREST MARATHON
00 40 94 588 813
www.bucharestmarathon.ro

RUSSIA
LUBJANSKI MARATHON
00 386 143 4 7598
www.slo-timing.org/marathon
MOSCOW MARATHON
00 7 095 924 0824
www.marafon.msk.ru

SERBIA
NOVI SAD MARATHON
00 381 21 51742
www.marathon.org.yu

SLOVAKIA
KOSICE PEACE MARATHON
00 421 55 622 0010
www.mmm.sk

SPAIN
BARCELONA MARATHON
00 34 93 268 0114
www.redestb.es/marathon_cat
MADRID MARATHON
00 34 902 210 578
www.mapoma.es
SEVILLE MARATHON
00 34 95 459 6841
www.marasevi.interbook.net
VALENCIA MARATHON
00 34 96 346 0707
www.correcaminos.org

SWEDEN
GOTEBORG HALF MARATHON
00 46 31 772 7880
www.goteborgsvarvet.com
STOCKHOLM MARATHON
00 46 8 54 566 440
www.marathon.se/eng

SWITZERLAND
JUNGFRAU MARATHON
00 41 33 828 3737
www.jungfrau-marathon.ch
LAUSANNE MARATHON
00 41 21 806 3016
www.lausanne-marathon.com
ZURICH MARATHON
00 41 1 480 2555
www.zurichmarathon.com

TURKEY
ISTANBUL EURASIA MARATHON
00 90 312 310 7652
www.taf.org.tr

YUGOSLAVIA
BELGRADE MARATHON
00 381 11 648 266
www.bgdmarathon.com

NORTH AMERICAN RACES:

BAA BOSTON MARATHON
001 508 435 6905
www.bostonmarthon.org
BIG SUR INTERNATIONAL MARATHON
001 831 625 6226
www.bsim.org
CASINO NIAGARA INTERNATIONAL
001 905 356 9460
www.discoverniagara.com
DEATH VALLEY BORAX MARATHON
001 415 868 1829
www.envirosports.com
HONOLULU MARATHON
001 808 734 7200
www.honolulumarathon.org
LAKE TAHOE MARATHON
001 530 544 7095
www.laketahoemarathon.com

LAS VEGAS MARATHON
001 702 240 2722
www.lvmarathon.com
LASALLE BANK CHICAGO MARATHON
001 312 904 9800
www.chicagomarathon.com
MARINE CORPS MARATHON
001 703 784 2225
www.marinemarathon.com
MAUI MARATHON
001 808 871 6441
www.mauimarathon.com
NATIONAL CAPITAL MARATHON
001 613 234 221
www.ncm.ca
NEW YORK CITY MARATHON
001 212 860 4455
www.nycmarathon.org
PORTLAND MARATHON
001 503 248 1134
www.portlandmarathon.org
QUEBEC CITY MARATHON
001 418 694 4442
www.marathonquebec.com
ROYAL VICTORIA MARATHON
001 250 658 4520
www.royalvictoriamarathon.com
SEATTLE MARATHON
001 206 729 3660
www.seattlemarathon.org
TORONTO MARATHON
001 416 972 1062
www.runtoronto.com
TORONTO WATERFRONT MARATHON
001 416 250 7700
www.runnerschoice.com
VANCOUVER INTERNATIONAL MARATHON
001 604 872 2928
www.adidasvanmarathon.ca

OTHER RACES:

AMAGASAKI MARATHON (JAPAN)
0081 6 6343 3564
ANGKOR WAT INTL HALF MARATHON
00 855 835 335
ANTARCTICA MARATHON
001 617 242 7845
www.marathontour.com

BANGKOK MARATHON
00 66 2 276 3605
www.amazingfield-tha.org
BEIJING INTL MARATHON
00 86 10 8676 1255
www.chinaaa.net
BOGOTA INTL HALF MARATHON
00 57 1 531 1860
www.Correcaminoscolombia.com
BUENOS AIRES CITY HALF MARATHON
www.amaisonproducciones.com.ar
COBAN INTL HALF MARATHON
00 502 634 0872
www.sportsandmarketing.net
COSTA RICA INTL MARATHON
00 506 258 3608
EGYPTIAN MARATHON
00 20 2 260 6900
www.egyptianmarathon.com
EVEREST MARATHON
01539 445 445
www.everestmarathon.org.uk
FLORA SYDNEY MARATHON
0061 28907 9475
www.sydneymarathon.org
GOLD COAST MARATHON
0061 75564 8733
www.goldcoastmarathon.com.au
GRAN MARATON PACIFICO (MAZATLAN)
00 525 281 0114
www.maraton.org
GREAT WALL MARATHON
00 45 51 50 6039
www.great-wall-marathon.com
GUAYAQUIL HALF MARATHON
www.elcorrecorre.com
HONG KONG MARATHON
00 852 2577 0800
www.hkmarathon.com
KILIMANJARO INTL MARATHON
00 27 11 974 7907
www.augrabiesextreme.cjb.net
MACAU INTERNATIONAL MARATHON
00 853 580 762
www.sport.gov.mo
MARABANA MARATHON (CUBA)
00 53 7 545 022
MEXICO CITY INTERNATIONAL MARATHON
00 525 5688 6829
www.maraton.df.gob.mx

MT MERU INTERNATIONAL MARATHON
00 255 22 264 7053
PANAMA CITY INTL MARATHON
00 507 260 6429
www.panamamarathon.com
POLAR CIRCLE MARATHON (GREENLAND)
0045 36 98 000
www.polar-circle-marathon.com
REGGAE MARATHON (JAMAICA)
001 876 967 1072
www.reggaemarathon.com
RIO MARATHON
0055 21 2244 3300
www.meiamaratonario.com.br
RUN BARBADOS MARATHON
001 416 250 7700
www.runbarbados.com
SAHARA MARATHON
001 703 969 0049
www.saharamarthon.org
SAO PAULO MARATHON
0055 11 5072 8006
www.maratonadesaopaulo.com.br
SIBERIAN MARATHON
007 3812 242 567
www.sim.omsknet.ru
SINGAPORE INTL MARATHON
00 65 6340 9607
www.singaporemarathon.com
TIBET MARATHON (LADAKH, INDIA)
0045 51 50 6039
www.great-tibetan-marathon.com
TWO OCEANS 56KM MARATHON
00 27 21 671 9407
www.TwoOceansMarathon.org.za
WORLD'S BEST 10KM (PUERTO RICO)
001 787 767 9191
www.worldbest10k.com

UK TOUR OPERATORS:

LEISURE PURSUITS GROUP
Essex House, Essex Road
Basingstoke, HANTS RG21 8SU
Tel: 01256 471 016
Fax: 01256 471 018
Email: reservations@leisurepursuits.com
www.leisurepursuits.com

SPORTS RESORT
2 The Parade, Cloughfields Road
Hoyland, S YORKS S74 0HR
Tel: 01226 741 741
Fax: 01226 741 742
Email: info@sportsresort.net

SPORTS TOURS INTERNATIONAL
91 Walkden Road, Walkden
MANCHESTER M28 7BQ
Tel: 0161 703 8161
Fax: 0161 703 8547
Email:
vince@sportstoursinmternational.co.uk
www.sportstoursinternational.co.uk

ASSOCIATIONS:

BRITISH ASSOCIATION OF ROAD RACES
01934 629911
BRITISH MASTERS ATHLETICS FEDERATION
020 8683 2602
TRAIL RUNNING ASSOCIATION
0118 987 2736
FELL RUNNING ASSOCIATION
01539 731012
UK ATHLETICS
0121 456 5098
SOUTH OF ENGLAND ATHLETIC
ASSOCIATION
020 8664 7244
MIDLAND COUNTIES ATHLETIC
ASSOCIATION
0121 452 1500
NORTH OF ENGLAND ATHLETIC
ASSOCIATION
0113 246 1835
ATHLETIC ASSOCIATION OF WALES
01633 416633
SCOTTISH ATHLETIC FEDERATION
0131 317 7320
NORTHERN IRELAND ATHLETIC
ASSOCIATION
02890 602707
NATIONAL SPORTS MEDICINE INSTITUTE
OF UK
020 7908 3636
LONDON SCHOOL OF SPORTS MASSAGE
020 8452 8855

Racing Calendar

The marathon calendar is growing every year, and you can be sure there is one which suits your schedule. When entering a marathon, book things such as air tickets and accommodation well in advance.

JANUARY

TIBERIAS MARATHON (Israel)
DUBAI (United Arab Emirates)
HONG KONG HALF MARATHON
CHINA COAST MARATHON (Hong Kong)
PACIFIC SHORELINE MARATHON (USA)
CHARLOTTE OBSERVER (USA)
WALT DISNEY WORLD (USA)
ENGLEWOOD RESERVE (USA)
KING DAY CLASSIC (USA)
POINT REYES CLASSIC (USA)
HOUSTEN – METHODIST (USA)
MARDI GRAS (USA)
GREAT VALLEY (USA)
RARITAN VALLEY (USA)
SAN DIEGO (USA)
WINTER FUN (USA)
BEARGREASE SHOWSHOE (USA)
ELLERBE SPRINGS (USA)
BERMUDA (USA)
TRINIDAD/TOBAGO (West Indies)
VIETNAM MARATHON
OSAKA INTERNATIONAL LADIES (Japan)

FEBRUARY

LAS VEGAS MARATHON
VALENCIA MARATHON
EGYPTIAN MARATHON (Luxor)
HONG KONG MARATHON
SEVILLE MARATHON
WORLD'S BEST 10KM (Puerto Rico)
SAHARA MARATHON
STINSON BEACH (USA)
TALLAHASSEE (USA)
MID-WINTER (USA)

CAROLINA (USA)
TYBEE (USA)
DFATH VALLEY TRAIL (USA)
LAS VEGAS INTERNATIONAL (USA)
LOST SOLES (USA)
METRO-DADE (USA)
CHARLOTTE OBSERVER (USA)
AUSTIN (USA)
OHIO RIVER RRC (USA)
SNOWFLAKE (USA)
VALLEY OF THE SUN (USA)
WASHINGTON'S BIRTHDAY (USA)
BLUE ANGEL (USA)
COWTOWN (USA)
SMOKY MOUNTAIN (USA)
HUDSON MOHAWK (USA)
OLYMPAID MEMORIAL (USA)
ESCAPE FROM MARIN (USA)
BEPPU – OITA MAINICHI (Japan)
VALENCIA (Spain)
CARIB CEMENT (Jamaica)
CAPETOWN (South Africa)
CIUDAD DE SEVILLA (Spain)
INTERNATIONAL EGYPTIAN (Egypt)

MARCH

KILIMANJARO MARATHON
ANTARCTICA MARATHON*
BARCELONA MARATHON
LISBON HALF MARATHON
PRAGUE HALF MARATHON
ROME MARATHON
MARSEILLE MARATHON
NOVI SAD HALF MARATHON
CITY PIER CITY HALF (Holland)
NANTUCKET (USA)

TRAIL'S END (USA)
B AND A TRAIL (USA)
HYANNIS, (USA)
LOS ANGELES (USA)
MENDOCINO TRAIL (USA)
NAPA VALLEY (USA)
MARCH MADNESS (USA)
MAUI (USA)
BIG BASIN REDWOODS (USA)
CATALINA (USA)
MUSIC CITY (USA)
SHAMROCK (USA)
SUFFOLK COUNTY (USA)
GREAT SOUTHWEST (USA)
TRAIL BREAKER (USA)
ATHENS (Greece)
LAKE BIWA MAINICHI (Japan)
CHINA COAST (China)
LAKE SIMCOE (Canada)
NAGOYA INTL WOMENS (Japan)
TEL AVIV (Israel)
CATALUNYA (Spain)
VUGARANO (Italy)
DONG-A-INTERNATIONAL (Korea)

APRIL

PARIS MARATHON
BERLIN HALF MARATHON
ROTTERDAM MARATHON
LONDON MARATHON
TURIN MARATHON
LISBON MARATHON
ZURICH MARATHON
NAGANO MARATHON (Japan)
BOSTON MARATHON
TWO OCEANS 56KM (South Africa)

HAMBURG MARATHON
BIG SUR MARATHON (USA)
WROCLAW MARATHON (Poland)
MADRID MARATHON
GOLDEN GATE-HEADLANDS (USA)
ARMY MULE MOUNTAIN (USA)
HOGEYE (USA)
BOSTON (USA)
CAMP LEJEUNE (USA)
HIGH PLAINS (USA)
LONGEST DAY (USA)
NAPA VALLEY TRAIL (USA)
GLASS CITY (USA)
PINE LINE TRAIL (USA)
ARMY (USA)
LAKE COUNTY (USA)
MICHIGAN TRAIL (USA)
AALBORG (Denmark)
BELGRADE (Yugoslavia)
BRASILIA (Brazil)
VIENNA CITY (Austria)

MAY

VANCOUVER MARATHON
BERLIN 25KM
GOTEBORG HALF MARATHON
COPENHAGEN MARATHON
COBAN HALF MARATHON (Guatemala)
GREAT WALL MARATHON
PRAGUE MARATHON
VIENNA MARATHON
NATIONAL CAPITAL (Ottawa, Canada)
GREAT POTATO (USA)
SHIPROCK (USA)
WHISKEY ROW (USA)
AVENUE OF THE GIANTS (USA)
BUFFALO (USA)
CITY OF PITTSBURGH (USA)
CLEVELAND (USA)
LINCOLN (USA)
LONG ISLAND (USA)
SPRING FLING (USA)
RACE OF CHAMPIONS (USA)
WILD WILD WEST (USA)
HEADLANDS WOLF RIDGE (USA)
LAKE GENEVA (USA)
MUIR WOODS (USA)
CAPITAL CITY (USA)
ANDY PAYNE (USA)

BAYSHORE (USA)
GAGE ROADRUNNER (USA)
LONG STAR PAPER CHASE (USA)
COEUR D'ALENE (USA)
MADISON (USA)
MED- CITY (USA)
VERMOUNT CITY (USA)
WYOMING (USA)
FLETCHER CHALLENGE (New Zealand)
FOREST CITY (Canada)
JOHNNY MILES (Canada)
TALLINN (Estonia)
TURIN (Italy)
OKANAGAN (Canada)
LAKELAND RUNAWAY (Canada)
MUNICH (Germany)

JUNE

MIDNIGHT SUN (TROMSO, Norway)
STOCKHOLM MARATHON
COMRADES 89KM (South Africa)
PAAVO NURMI MARATHON (Finland)
GOD'S COUNTRY (USA)
COVERNOR'S CUP (USA)
RIDGERUNNER (USA)
GOLD COUNTRY TRAIL (USA)
NIPMUCK TRAIL (USA)
STEAMBOAT (USA)
PALOS VERDES (USA)
SUNBURST (USA)
HOOSIER (USA)
SUGARLOAF (USA)
TAOS (USA)
VALLEY OF THE FLOWERS (USA)
MARATHON TO MARATHON (USA)
FILA SKY (USA)
HIGH SIERRA (USA)
GRANDMA'S (USA)
MAYOR'S MIDNIGHT SUN (USA)
PARK OF ROSES (USA)
MARATHON DELA BAIC DES (Canada)
MELBOURNE (Australia)
YUKON GOLD MIDNIGHT (Canada)
MANITOBA (Canada)
TWENTE (Holland)
MIDNIGHT SUN (Canada)
MOUNT KILIMANJARO (Africa)

JULY

GOLD COAST MARATHON (Australia)
GUAYAQUIL HALF MARATHON (Ecuador)
TALLINN MARATHON (Estonia)
SAO PAULO MARATHON (Brazil)
CALGARY STAMPEDE (Canada)
PAAVO NURMI (Finland)
FRIENDLY VOYAGEUR (Canada)
HELSINKI CITY (Finland)
NOVA SCOTIA (Canada)
GRANDFATHER MOUNTAIN (USA)
OHIO/MICHIGAN (USA)
SAN FRANCISCO (USA)
MOSQUITO (USA)
UNIVERSITY OF OKOBOJI (USA)
DESERET NEWS (USA)
KILAUEA VOLCANO (USA)

AUGUST

SIBERIAN MARATHON (Omsk)
MOUNT MERU MARATHON (Arusha)
HELSINKI MARATHON
BOGOTA HALF MARATHON
PANAMA MARATHON
GREAT TIBETAN MARATHON (India)
REYKJAVIK MARATHON
RIO DE JANEIRO HALF MARATHON
QUEBEC MARATHON
DRAKES BAY TRAIL (USA)
CRATER LAKE RIM (USA)
FRANK MAIER (USA)
PAAVO NURMI (USA)
MAMMOUNTH MOUNTAIN TRAIL (USA)
SUMMER SPREE (USA)
PIKES PEAK (USA)
UNION INTERNATIONAL (USA)
KONA (USA)
SILVER STATE (USA)
SAUSALITO (USA)
FESTIVAL-BY-THE-SEA (Canada)
DAIHATSU ADELAIDE (Australia)
EDMONTON FESTIVAL (Canada)

SEPTEMBER

JUNGFRAU MARATHON (Switzerland)
BUDAPEST HALF MARATHON
MOSCOW MARATHON

BUENOS AIRES HALF MARATHON
GREAT SCOTTISH RUN HALF (Glasgow)
PILA HALF MARATHON (Poland)
SYDNEY MARATHON
POLAR CIRCLE MARATHON
BRISTOL HALF MARATHON
MEDOC MARATHON (France)
NOVI SAD MARATHON (Yugoslavia)
MAUI MARATHON
TALLINN HALF MARATHON
TURIN HALF MARATHON
TORONTO WATERFRONT MARATHON
ROBIN HOOD MARATHON
PORTUGAL HALF MARATHON
ROUTE DU VIN HALF (Luxembourg)
BERLIN MARATHON
BLACK HILLS (USA)
MONSTER TRAILS (USA)
SCOTTY HANTON (USA)
SNOWGOOSE (USA)
TUPELO (USA)
HEART OF AMERICA (USA)
TURTLE (USA)
AMERICAN ODYSSEY (USA)
BISMARCK (USA)
JACKSON (USA)
MUIR BEACH TRAIL (USA)
DUTCHESS COUNTY (USA)
MARATHON OF THE ROSES (USA)
NORTHERN SHUFFLERS (USA)
BURNEY CLASSIC (USA)
ERIESISTIBLE (USA)
BETHEL MOUNTAIN (USA)
EQUINOX (USA)
SUGAR RIVER TRAIL (USA)
WALKER NORTH (USA)
FALL FANTASY (USA)
CLARENCE DEMAR (USA)
DUKE CITY (USA)
EAST LYME (USA)
PORTLAND (USA)
BEAVERLODGE – GRAND PRARIE (Canada)
TWIN CITIES (Canada)
GOLDEN EAGLE (Canada)
OILSANDS (Canada)
SASKATCHEWAN (Canada)
YELLOWKNIFE (Canada)
AMSTERDAM CITY (Holland)
MONTREAL (Canada)
PRINCE EDWARD ISLAND (Canada)

OCTOBER

BUCHAREST MARATHON
KOSICE MARATHON (Slovakia)
PORTLAND MARATHON
LAKE TAHOE MARATHON
CHICAGO MARATHON
ROYAL VICTORIA MARATHON
AMSTERDAM MARATHON
BEIJING MARATHON
BEIRUT MARATHON
LUBJANSKI MARATHON (Slovakia)
ISTANBUL MARATHON
MEXICO CITY MARATHON
TORONTO MARATHON
NIAGARA MARATHON
LAUSANNE MARATHON
MARINE CORPS MARATHON
VENICE MARATHON
DUBLIN MARATHON
NEW HAMPSHIRE (USA)
ORCAS ISLAND TRAIL (USA)
ST GEORGE (USA)
FOX CITIES (USA)
JOHNSTOWN (USA)
MAINE (USA)
SACRAMENTO (USA)
TWIN CITIES (USA)
WINEGLASS (USA)
YONKERS (USA)
CITY OF GALLUP (USA)
HARTFORD (USA)
ATLANTIC CITY (USA)
BARTON ROUGE BEACH (USA)
GREATER KANSAS CITY (USA)
BAY STATE (USA)
LAKEFRONT (USA)
PUEBLO RIVER TRAIL (USA)
RICHMOND (USA)
STREAMTOWN (USA)
TOE TO TOW TRAIL (USA)
CAESAR CREEK (USA)
GREEN MOUNTAIN (USA)
WHICHITA (USA)
CHICAGO (USA)
COLORADO (USA)
DETROIT FREE PRESS (USA)
HUMBOLDT REDWOODS (USA)
MOHAWK – HUDSON RIVER (USA)
ST. LOUIS (USA)

SKYLINE TO THE SEA TRAIL (USA)
CAPE COD (USA)
MARINE CORPS (USA)
TWIN LAKES (Canada)
CANADIAN INTERNATIONAL (Canada)
VALLEY HARVEST (Canada)
ATHENS (Greece)
FRANKFURT (Germany)
ITALIAN INTERNATIONAL (Italy)

NOVEMBER

NEW YORK CITY MARATHON
ATHENS CLASSIC MARATHON
MARABANA (LA HAVANA) MARATHON
MONACO MARATHON
AMAGASAKI MARATHON (Japan)
FIRENZE MARATHON
MALTA CHALLENGE MARATHON (3 days)
BANGKOK MARATHON
GRAN MARATON PACIFICO (Mexico)
SEATTLE MARATHON
ANDREW JACKSON (USA)
ARKANSAS (USA)
BIG SUR TRAIL (USA)
CHEROKEE STRIP (USA)
MORGAN HILL (USA)
LEPRECHAUN (USA)
NEW YORK CITY (USA)
OCEAN STATE (USA)
OMAHA RIVER (USA)
WARWICK (USA)
CHICAMAUGA BATTLEFIELD (USA)
CITY OF SANTA CLARITA (USA)
COLUMBUS (USA)
HAMPDEN-SYDNEY (USA)
HARRISBURG (USA)
SAN ANTONIO (USA)
VULCAN (USA)
PALM DESERT (USA)
PHILADELPHIA (USA)
TULSA (USA)
HOLIDAY (USA)
SEATTLE (USA)
SPACE COAST (USA)
ATLANTA (USA)
MISSISSIPPI BEACH (USA)
NORTHERN CENTRAL TRAIL (USA)
AMSTERDAM CITY (Holland)
ADIDAS (Argentina)

DECEMBER

REGGAE MARATHON (JAMAICA)
COSTA RICA MARATHON
SINGAPORE MARATHON
BARBADOS MARATHON
DEATH VALLEY MARATHON
MACAU MARATHON
ANGKOR WAT HALF MARATHON
HONOLULU MARATHON
ALMOST HEAVEN (USA)
BULLDOG (USA)
DALLAS WHITE ROCK (USA)
FIESTA BOWL (USA)
HOLIDAY (USA)
MEMPHIS (USA)
WESTERN HEMISPHERE (USA)
ALAMAGORDO (USA)
KENTUCKY (USA)
MISSISSIPPI (USA)
BRANDON (USA)
CALIFORNIA INTERNATIONAL (USA)
CHRISTMAS (USA)
DELAWARE (USA)
HONOLULU (Hawaii)
TUCSON (USA)
JACKSONVILLE (USA)
KIAWAH ISLAND (USA)
ROCKET CITY (USA)
MARATHON SIX-PACK (USA)
NEW YEARS RESOLUTION TRAIL (USA)
MACAU (South China)

Index